PANCHAYATI RAJ SYSTEM IN INDIA

PANCHAYATI RAJ SYSTEM IN INDIA

S. DHARMARAJ

ABHIJEET PUBLICATIONS
DELHI 110094

ABHIJEET PUBLICATIONS
2/46 Tukhmeerpur Extension
Delhi-110 094
Phone: 011-22960492 (Fax), 65698474
E-mail: abhijeetpublication@gmail.com

PANCHAYATI RAJ SYSTEM IN INDIA

First Published 2008

ISBN 978-81-89886-78-3

PRINTED IN INDIA

Published by J.K. Singh for Abhijeet Publications, Delhi-110 094, Lasertypeset by Gaurav Graphics, New Delhi and Printed at Himanshu Printers, Delhi.

Dedicated
to
My Parents

M. SENGAMALAM
M. KAMALAM

Preface

Gandhiji wanted to achieve Swaraj, it is possible only by means of Decentralised Planning. Since devolution of powers between Central, State and local governments is the need of the hour today in a prompt manner. Nagarpalika bills, 73rd Amendment to Constitution envisage giving more autonomy to local bodies.

Panchayati Raj System is definitely a boon to the rural and far flung areas so as to achieve desired results in the Gram Panchayat environment in India.

This book made on attempt to analyse the orgin, growth and latest developments in the arena of panchayatraj system. It also gives a bird's eye view of decentralised planning. Hence the real progress of panchayat raj system depends upon only the people's participation in Rural Development.

S. DHARMARAJ

Acknowledgements

I am extremely thankful to T.A. Julius, former Head of the Department of Eeconomic, Nehru Memorial College, Puthanampatti for his support and encouragement throughout for writing this book.

I owe my sincere thanks to R. Manimekalai, Head of the department in economics, Nehru Memorial College, Puthanampatti for her timely help.

I am greatly indebted to Dr. V. Selvaraj, Reader in Commerce, Nehru Memorial College, Puthanampatti for his constant encouragement.

My special thanks to Dr. D. Kumar, Department of Economic, Jamal Mohammed College, Tiruchirapalli, Dr. S. Murugan, Department of Economics, EVR College, Thiurchirapalli and Mr. K. Palanivel, Prof. EVR College, Thiruchirapalli for helping me in all matters of the book information.

I take this opportunity to express my heartfelt thanks to my beloved colleagues, P. Rasamahendran, Mr.

M.R.Karuppaiah, A. Shanmugam, Dr. V. Murugesan for their constructive criticism in this work.

I owe my affectionate thanks to my beloved friends Mr. A. Sekar, Mr. K. Thiagarajan, Mr. V. Senthilkumar for their enthusiastic help.

I feel happy to thank my in–laws Mrs. & Mr. A. Eswaran and Mrs. and Mr. Lakshmi Narayanan Software Engineer, Hyderabad, Mr. Murugapandian, Project Manager, Chennai and Mrs. E. Maithili, Lecturer Computer Science S.A. Engineering College, Chennai.

Without their constant pressure and cooperation, I would not have visited centers of learning for data collection.

I would be failing in my duty if I could express my profound thanks to my wife Mrs. Lalitha senior lecturer in chemistry, M.A.M., College of Engineering Tiruchirapalli and to sons Keerthivasan and Thiru. Srinivasan for their timely help in bringing this book in time.

My profound thanks to my beloved sisters Jayalakshmi Muthukannu, Bhagyalakshmi and Umarani who helped me in many ways.

I owe my sincere thanks to my mentor Mr. S. Palanimuthu, M.A., B.Ed., (Retd. Teacher) and Mrs. Kamatchi for the moral support and financial support to take up this project.

I am thankful to Abhijeet Publications, Delhi for their interest and coöperation in publishing this book.

S. DHARMARAJ

Contents

Preface *vii*

Acknowledgements *ix*

1. Structural Pattern of Panchayati Raj in India 1
2. Perspective on Decentralisation 18
3. Panchayati Raj, Development and Developmental Performance: An Institution Building Perspective 43
4. Responsive Administration and Panchayati Raj 106
5. Reflections on Panchayati Raj 126

Bibliography 165

Index 169

1

Structural Pattern of Panchayati Raj in India

The Structural patterns of Panchayati Raj in India, as we find them today are varied and complex. The ideal is everywhere the same and the basic objectives are identical, but the shape and forms do not follow quite the same pattern. There are departures, variations and innovations here and there. These roots are traceable to the basic pattern recommended by the Balwantrai Mehta Report. The key passage in the terms of reference (laid down by the Planning Commission, which appointed the Committee on Plan Projects) read: "to study and report on the Community Projects and the national extension service with a view to economy and efficiency with special reference to problems connected with the organic linking of the village Panchayats with popular organizations at a higher level; and by stages determined in advance, the reorganization of district administration so that democratic bodies could takeover the entire general administration and development of the district, or the sub-division, other than such functions as law and order, administration of justice and certain functions pertaining to the revenue administration.

The Central Council of Local Self Government in its fifth meeting held at Hyderabad in 1959 took stock of the action taken by the states to implement the PR and recommended that while the broad pattern and the fundamentals may be uniform, there should not be any rigidity in the pattern. In fact, the country is so large and Panchayati Raj is so complex a subject with far reaching consequences, that there is the fullest scope for trying out various patterns and alternatives. What is most important is the genuine transfer of power to the people. If this is ensured, form and pattern may necessarily vary according to conditions prevailing in different states. The Government of India have largely followed this policy and the states have been allowed to evolve patterns of PR suitable to local conditions in the light of certain broad principles.

Organization Structure

In the initial stages PR was implemented enthusiastically starting with Rajasthan and Andhra Pradesh (1959). Later it was introduced in a number of other states. A notable aspect of the evolution of PR in early sixties was the way two states—Maharashtra and Gujarat—not only accepted the idea of PR, but also innovated a Strong tier at the district level. These two pioneers of a strong Zilla Parishad pattern have remained the best examples of PR in the country. In the Nineties three other states, West Bengal, Andhra Pradesh and Karnataka, have shown great interest in making these bodies more powerful. The three institutions—Panchayat at the village level. Panchayat Samiti at the block level and Zilla Parishad at the district level-are interlinked and form part of the same structure. However, the inter-relationship between them is a variable phenomenon.

Shiviah highlighted that outside the pioneering states of Rajasthan, Andhra Pradesh, Maharashtra and Gujarat, the progress of PR in several other states was marked by prevarications. He further mentioned 'there were other regions too, where acceptance of the Mehta Scheme in to involved some difficulties. In the south, Kerala, with its characteristically long stretches of continuous settlements involving bigger Gram Panchayats, did not find the Panchayat Samiti a feasible proposition. In the then Madras (Tamil Nadu) a new course was charted after the submission of the Mehta Committee Report, in that the Panchayat Union Councils were constituted at the block level and the district Development Councils at the district level (1958). The states in the North Eastern region presented an altogether different picture; with tribal councils. In Bihar, a three-tier pattern was introduced, but the district level body was established in only 8 of the 31 districts. In Madhya Pradesh, a law providing for a three-tier structure was passed in 1962, but fact the Zilla Parishads were not established. Uttar Pradesh went in for the Rajasthan, Andhra Pradesh Pattern, but it did not show comparable enthusiasm . In Punjab and Orissa, what was in effect a two-tier system did not fare very well. Haryana abolished the upper tier (Zilla Parishad) in 1973 and is now having only two tiers. And Jammu and Kashmir has been, by and large, content with only one tier, that of village Panchayats.

PR has had a chequred growth in a number of states. A more interesting development is the abolition of the district level body subsequently in two states: Orissa and Haryana. The West Bengal Panchayat Act of 1974 reduces the number of tiers from four to three. Assam has reduced the number of tiers to two retaining the top Mahkuma level. The latest tally of three and two-tier systems is as follows:

Three–tier: Andhra Pradesh, Arunachal Pradesh, Bihar, Gujarat, Hi-machal Pradesh, Karnataka, Madhya Pradesh, Manipur, Maharashtra, Punjab, Rajasthan, TamilNadu, Uttar Pradesh and West Bengal.

Two-tier: Assam, Haryana, Jammu & Kasmir, Kerala, Orissa and Sikkim.

In Orissa, efforts are being made to reintroduce Zilla Parishads. It may be noted that the powers and functions of gram Panchayats being broadly similar throughout the country, a basic issue in the structural pattern of PR is the elative strength of the Zilla Parishad and the Panchayat Samiti. With regard to the six states listed under the category of 'two-tier pattern' above, the district-level body being not in existence, the block level body is, of course, quite powerful. However, in the three-tier category we find considerable variation. Shiviah's classification given below continues to hold good.

1. In Maharashtra, the Zilla Parishad is very strong, overshadowing the Samiti which performs agency functions. In Gujarat, though the Zilla Parishad is powerful, the Taluka Panchayat fares relatively better compared to its counterpart in Maharashtra.
2. In Tamil Nadu, Punjab and Rajasthan, the district level body has merely 'advisory' functions.

3. In Andhra Pradesh, Bihar, Himachal Pradesh, Rajasthan, Uttar Pradesh and West Bengal, the district level body is less powerful than in category, but more powerful than in category.

Coverage of Panchayati Raj

The statistics relating to the distribution of PR Institutions in the country are fairly impressive. PR is now under implementation in almost all the states of India. The number of villages covered by the PR Institutions in the country as a whole is 5,53,668 with 2,17,300 Panchayats in the country. The population covered by these bodies is 4618.56 lakhs which forms 99.6 percent of the total rural population. On an average 2,306 persons are covered by each Panchayat at the lower level. The highest coverage of the population per Gram Panchayat is in the State of Assam (24,065) followed by Kerala (20,661) whereas the lowest coverage s in Punjab (1109). Amongs the UTS, Dadra and Nagar Haveli cover the maximum number of persons (10,300) per Gram Panchayat vis-à-vis the lowest coverage of 1,381 persons in Chandigarh. The existing Panchayat Samitis in the country are 4,528 which is 90 percent of the number of total CD blocks. On an average 50.5 Gram Panchayats are covered per Panchyat Samiti. The Coverage is the highest in Punjab (92.81) followed by U.P. (82.8) and the lowest is in West Bengal (10.0). The total number of Zilla Parishads functioning in the country is 344 (including Kerala) and the average number of Panchayat Samitis per Zilla Parishad is 11.2, the maximum being in West Bengal (22.6) and the minimum in Chandigarh (1.0).

As the figures reflect PR Institutions have got universal coverage. All the States and union Territories have opted for these bodies, if not all the tiers, at least Gram Panchayats and Panchayat Samitis suited to local conditions are existing. The Tribal council set up in the North-Eastern region is protected by a separate set of provisions in the constitution. A few Union Territories too come under this category.

In the following pages, an attempt is made to give a brief account of the system in force in different states, bringing out the major points of similarity and pointing out the major variations.

Different Nomenclature

There is some ticklish difference in the nomenclature of various institutions and functionaries. There is no substantial difference about the village level body—it is generally known as Gram or Gram Panchayat. However the intermediary body at the block or taluk level bears many names. The Balwantrai Mehta Committee suggested 'Panchayat Samiti' for its name and the same has been adopted by ten states, but in Assam, it is known as 'Anchalik Panchayat', in Madhya Pradesh, Janpad Panchayat, in Tamilnadu, Panchayat Union Council, in Gujarat, Taluka Panchayat, Anchalik Samit in Arunachal Pradesh. In Andhra Pradesh, Mandal Praja Parishad, in Karnataka, Taluka Panchayat Samit and Kshetra Samiti in U.P. similarly, the district level body (except in Assam) is generally known as Zilla Parishad but Andhra Pradesh calls it zilla Praja Parishad, in Gujarat it is 'District Panchayat', in Madhya Pradesh 'Zilla Panchayat', and in Kerala, 'District Council'. Assam has sub-divisional bodies known as Mohkuma Parishad.

More crucial than this is the nomenclature of the functionaries. The Chairman of the Gram Panchayat is known as 'Sarpanch' in Andhra Pradesh, Gujarat, Haryana, Maharashtra, Orissa, Punjab, and Rajasthan; and President' in Assam, Kerala, Mizoram and Tamil Nadu and "Pradhan' in the rest of the states. The head of the Panchayat Samiti is called 'Chairman' in Haryana Himachal Pradesh, Karnataka, Madhya Pradesh, Maharashtra, Orissa, Punjab and Tamil Nadu; 'President' in Andhra Pradesh, Arunachal Pradesh and Gujarat. In Bihar, Manipur and Uttar Pradesh, he is known as 'Pramukh'. Whereas, in Rajasthan and West Bengal the head is named as Pradhan and Sabhapati, respectively. At the apex level, the head of the Zilla Parishad is designated as 'Chairman' in Andhra Pradesh, Himachal Pradesh, Punjab and Uttar Pradesh; in Arunachal Pradesh, Gujarat, Maharashtra and Manipur, as 'President' ; in Bihar and Karnataka, the head is designated as 'Adhyaksha'; he is called 'Sabhapati', 'Sabhadhipati; and Zilla Pramukh in Madhya Pradesh, West Bengal and Rajasthan, respectively. In fact, these terms are quite confusing. In Rajasthan, the head of the Panchayat Samiti is Pradhan whereas in Uttar Pradesh, he is called Pradhan at Panchayat level, and Pramukh at Panchayat Samiti level. Likewise in Madhya Pradesh, Sabhapati is the head of the Zilla Parishad and n West Bengal Sabhapati is the head of the Panchayat Samit. This arbitrary use of the same terms in different meaning by two or more states adds to the confusion. To get over this problem it would be appropriate to have a uniform nomenclature throughout the country.

Composition of PRIs

Gram Panchayat. The general pattern of the composition of the PRIs is based on the principle of democracy and the predominance of the elected members. However, there is also provision for *ex-officio,* co-opted or nominated members. The Balwantrai Mehta Committee had recommended that the Panchayat should be purely on an elected basis, but that there may be a provision for the cooption of two women members and one member each from the SC and ST in the conditions similar to those prescribed for Panchayt Samiti. In general, it has been followed in all states. The election is held on territorial basis and the Panchayat area is generally divided into a number of wards. The membership of the Panchayat varies between 5 and 25—Punjab has between 4-11, Rajasthan and Tamil Nadu between 5–15 and West Bengal between 7-25. The Sarpanch of Gram Panchayat is elected directly in Andhra Pradesh, Assam, Bihar, Gujarat, Haryana, Himachal Pradesh, Madhya Pradesh, Maharashtra, Manipur, Orissa, Punjab, Rajasthan, Tamil Nadu and Uttar Pradesh. He is elected by the members in the rest of the States. Bihar has a unique provision under which out of 9 members, 5 members including sarpanch are directly elected. The other four members are nominated by the Mukhiya to give adequate representation to women and other minorities. The Rajasthan Panchayat Act., 1953, provides for cooption of women and members of the SC and ST on certain conditions. In Punjab, seats are reserved for these categories. Some of the seats of Sarpanches in Andhra Pradesh are reserved for SC and ST persons. In Madhya Pradesh if any Panchayat is dominated by SC or ST the Sarpanch will be from those communities only.

The prevailing system of direct election of panchas by secret ballot in most of the states has been regarded as the best method by various study teams on Panchayati Raj. The Santhanam Committee on Panchayati Raj Elections (1965) observed that "all the members of the Panchayat, including representatives of women, SC/ST should be elected and there should be elected and there should be no coopted, nominated or ex-officio members. The ARC Study Team on District Administration also felt that all members of gram panchayat should be directly elected. The Vyas Committee (Rajasthan) observed that "cooption in fact is nothing bust a corrosion and infringement of true democratic process and the representatives of SC, ST and women getting a place through cooption in Panchayats, Panchayat Samitis or Zilla parishads are nothing but a creation of the generosity of members of these bodies and consequently their participation in the deliberations of such bodies is far from active or objective.

Panchayat Samiti. The Panchayat Samiti generally consists of representatives of the Panchayats, Cooperatives, small municipalities and notified area committees, Members of Legislative Assemblies and certain officers. Representation for women, SC and ST is usually secured by cooption. Instates like Gujarat, Karnataka and Maharashtra seats fro SC/ST are reserved on the basis of population and in the rest of the states minimum number is specified. Some posts of Chairmen are also reserved in Andhra Pradesh and Madhya Pradesh.

In Tamil Nadu, each Panchayat elects one representative to the Samit. In Punjab and Haryana, the Panchas and Sarpanchas in the Samiti area elect a prescribed number of members to the Samiti from amongst themselves. In U.P., Punjab, Madhya Pradesh and Gujarat, municipal bodies in the area are also represented in the Samiti. In all the states except Maharashtra, M.Ps and MLAs are members of this body. In Orissa only MLAs are members, butwith voting right. In U.P., they have a right to vote. Among the officials, BDO is an ex-officio member and executive secretary of the Panchayat Samiti.

The mode of election of the Samiti President has alsoattracted a good deal of attention. He is elected by the members of panchayat Samiti in most of the states except Andhra Pradesh. We may, in this connection, note that the Administrative Reforms Commission (1973) in Tamil Nadu, favoured direct election of the Chairman of the Panchayat Union Council. But the Study Team of the Adminsitrative Reforms Commission (1967), however, observed that the "Pradhan of the Samiti should be electedby an electoral collegeconsisting of the members of all Gram Panchayats. The Narasimham and Vyas Committees, also favoured the election of the President by the members on the ground that in the scheme visualized by them, the directly elected component would be quite large.

It is pertinent here to point out that there has developed a big terminological confusion in Panchayat Samiti. Besides, there is some difference in the nomenclature of Various functionaries. Thus, comparisons become difficult and some times misleading impressions can be gathered.

Zilla Parishad. The composition of the Zilla Parishad also follows the pattern of the Panchayat Samiti. In Gujarat and Punjab, Samiti members also elect a member in addition to the Chairman. In Arunachal Pradesh and Gujarat, provision has been made for direct election of members. In states like Bihar, Himachal Pradesh,

Karnataka, Madhya Pradesh, Maharashra, Manipur, Uttar Pradesh and West Bengal some members are directly elected, some are nominated and coopted. He Maharashtra Act (1962) Section 9 (1) (9) provides that the Zilla Parishad will consist of councilors chosen by direct election from electoral divisions in the district being not more than 60 in number and not less than 40 as may be notification in the official Gazette, be determined by the State Government so that there is one councillor as far as is reasonably practicable for not more than every thirty five thousand of the population. Thus , the Zilla Parishad becomes something like a district Legislature. In Maharashtra, it may be justify since the Parishad has been made powerful.

Beside special provision for the representation of women is made in all states except, Punjab and Tamilnadu. As we have already mentioned, in Andhra Pradesh, Karnataka and Kerala, reservation for women is 9, 25 and 3 percent respectively. Special representation to the SC and ST is also provided in all the state except Maharastra and Orissa. The chairman of the Zilla Parished is elected from among its members in a large number of states. Only in Andrapradesh, he is elected directly by the voters. The ARC study team preferred the election of the chairman by an electrol college consisting of members of the gram panchayats with in the jurisdiction of the Parishad. This election, in their opinion, should be held simultaneously with that of the Pradhan of the Panchayat Samiti. In the states were there is indirect election to this apex body of PR, direct election is favoured. In Andhra Pradesh, the Narasimham Committee suggested direct election for Zilla Parishad from single member constituencies (electrol circles) into which the Samiti blocks divided.

In Andhra Pradesh, 15,20 and 9 percent of the total numbers of officers of president in a district (excluding the number of officers reserved for STs in schedule area) are reserved for the SCs, BCs and women respectively by rotation, from term to term.

MPs and MLAs are *ex-officio* members of the Zilla Parishads in all the states except Maharashtra and Kerala. They have voting right in all states except Gujarat, Orissa, and Punjab. The association of MPs and MLAs as associate members with this body is a ontroversial problem. In the opinion of the Bongirwar Committee (Maharashtra), their association with Zilla Parishad is not necessary as "it would be anomalous to include the representatives of a higher body (the state legislature) in the lower body (the Zilla Parishad)". In Maharashtra and Kerala, they are kept out of the PR bodies.

The membership of Zilla Parishad is fairly large. In UP, it has about 70 members, Besides, districts do not have uniformity of size. In Rajasthan, one district has 4 Panchayat Samitis and another has as many as 7, there is a substantial difference about the mode of elections of Zilla Parishad members and Chairman. Besides, there are some variations in the reservation for women. Certain departures are noticeable about the role of MPs and MLAs. Too many variations make comparison very difficult and confusing.

Staffing Pattern

The bureaucracy that is connected with the PR can be broadly classified into two—generalists and technical officers. The Chief Executive Officers and BDOs perform functions of a general administrative nature. The district technical officers, e.g., District Agricultural Officer,

Executive Engineer and Extension Officers, Can be classified as the technical wing of the Panchayati Raj bureaucracy. At the village level, there is the VLM who is a multipurpose officer in charge of four or five villages (in some states he is known a village development officer). He is mainly concerned with development works in his jurisdiction and works under the general supervision and control of the Panchyat Samiti. In addition to the VLW, there is Secretary to look after the administrative work of the Panchayat Samiti, as is the case in Punjab, Haryana, Orissa and Kerala. Maharashtra and Gujarat have adopted a different system. In these two states, the *talathi* performs the functions of the VLW and the Secretary of the Panchyat.

At the block level, there is uniformity with regard to the staffing pattern. This is the result of the Panchayat Samiti having taken over the functions of the former Community Development Block. In all the states, the Chief Executive Officer is the BDO, who coordinates the work of the staff under him. He is drawn either from the revenue or some other development department. In some states, e.g. Punjab and Haryana, there is provision for the direct recruitment of the Block Development Officers. There is a great similarity in the functions which the BDO is to perform.

At the district level, different administrative arrangements exist in different states. There is a Chief Executive Officer or Secretary who is the Chief Executive of the Zilla Parishad. His nomenclature varies; he is known as the Chief Executive Officer in Maharashtra; the District Development Officer in Bihar, Gujarat, Andhra Pradesh and Punjab; Executive Officer in West Bengal (collector is the EO). In Karnataka, he is known as Chief Secretary. In some other states, he is either an

Additional collector or a District Development Officer; in other states he is of the rank of a Deputy Collector. To some extent, there is a correlation between the position of the Zilla Parishad and the position of the Chief Executive Officer of the Zilla Parishad.

Another aspect of the PR bureaucracy is the appointment on deputation terms. Most of the senior officers and technical staff are drawn from the state government as deputationists. Rami Reddy observed that this has an adverse effect. The deputationists feel that since they are not employees of the PR, they need not be fully loyal to them. They regards their stay in the PR institutions as purely temporary.

Committee System

Without a brief mention of the Committee System in PR, a discussion on its organization cannot be considered complete since the standing committees thereof play a vital role in its working. The committees relieve the main body from the burden of day-to-day routine work. Besides, there is greater scope to associate on members with skills in particular fields. Such association should help in securing better participation of the people. The Congress MPs' Study Team considered the existence of the standing committee as, 'a further decentralization of responsibility and power'.

The Committees have been provided in all the three institutions of PR, but their number and composition vary in different states. The number of committees of the Village Panchayat vary from one in Rajasthan to eight or more in Bihar and Maharashtra. States such as Haryana, Kerala, Orissa and Punjab have not specified the number of Committee a Panchayat should continue.

Tamil Nadu has no provision for the constitution of Committees.

The Panchayat Samiti also operates through its statuary Committees. Generally speaking they deal with:

(1) Production Programmes,

(2) Social Welfare,

(3) Cooperation, Cottage Industries, etc.,

(4) Education,

(5) Rural Water Supply, health and Sanitation,

(6) Communication and other allied subjects, and

(7) Finance, taxation and administration. The number of these committees varies from minimum three in Punjab to maximum eight in Bihar. The Statutory Committees exercise only the powers delegated by the Panchayat Samiti.

The Rajasthan Act provides for three types of Committees for Zilla Parishad Production programme, for finance, taxes and administration. Kerala provides for six committees at District Council—general, finance, development, welfare, public works and education. The Zilla Parishad in Uttar Pradesh also constitutes six committees for performance of various duties. Karya Samiti, Vitta Samiti, Shiksha Samiti, Sarvjanik Nirman Samiti, Jan Sawathya and Niyojan Samiti. Andhra Pradesh has six committees—development, education, social welfare, woman welfare, works and committee on finance. In Karnataka, a Zilla Parishad has none committees. Usually, Zilla Parishads constitute six or seven committees in which education, social welfare and finance are common. The pattern of heading these committees also differs from state to state. In Andhra Pradesh, the Chairman of the Zilla Parishad is the

Chairperson of all the Standing Committees. In certain states officials are made the Chairmen of these committees. In Rajasthan, however, the experience with non-official Chairman has been satisfactory. Between the committees themselves the predominance of the committee on administration and finance has been noticed. As man as 43 percent of the total meetings of the Standing committees in Rajasthan during a given period were related to finance and administration and 35 percent with production programmes.

Conclusion

From the foregoing account, it is evident that except for broad similarities on the basis and fundamental aspects, there are large and wide variations in the patterns of PR system operating in the various states of the country. The approach to this question has been practical and pragmatic so that each state could devise a system which is best suited to the PR institutions in the area, It may be noted that of the 20 states referred to above, as many as six states are classified under the two-tier category: Assaın, Haryana, Jammu & Kashmir, Kerala, Orissa and Sikkim. This is a significant departure from the Mehta scheme. Haryana and Orissa had a district level body earlier, but was abolished subsequently; Assam too did away with one tier, retaining however, the top tier at the Mahkuma level. Kerala has introduced District Council but the Act does not provide for middle level tier. In regard to the mode of election, participation of political parties in the election on the basis of symbol, nomenclature, reservation for women, association of MPs, MLAs, their right to vote and number of tiers in existence differ widely. Some of the states have provided for some representation to the adjoining municipalities also. Of course, PR Institutions have got good coverage. All the states and Union Territories have opted for these bodies, if not all the three tiers, at least gram panchayats and Panchayat Samitis suited to local conditions are existing.

2

Perspective on Decentralization

Over the last few years, there has been an emerging consensus-across political parties and ideological divisions-on the necessity of decentralization for fulfilling democratic aspirations of the Indian people. Despite differences in points of departure underlying this 'consensus' (as reflected in various party manifestos), it is a good time to go over the debate on decentralization that had preceded this consensus. I shall try to do this in this paper.

But before I do that, let me first state my own convictions. To me, it is clear that the only alternative to a decentralized and genuinely democratic political system in a country like India is the gradual dissipation, erosion and ultimate disintegration of the State as well as the nation. There have already been many signs of this- the power of the regional satraps has increased, parochial tendencies of region and caste are very much on the upsurge, at lower levels contractors and wheeler-dealers in money and muscle power are in command.

All in all, the authority of the Indian State is getting eroded-at all levels.

The corrective to such a state of affairs will need to be conceived in terms that are organic rather than mechanistic. The real case for decentralization rests no on the claims of territorial rights of juridical entities or political parties but on the comprehension, based on experience, that in a country like India, a centralized polity is incapable of dealing with an unjust social order, that it is inimical to the democratic political process, and that it is inherently unstable.

Under what conditions is national unity best promoted? By concentrating power and decision-making at the centre and increasing its capacity to determine national priorities and counter regional and local pulls and pressures or by evolving a framework of participation at various levels that is sensitizing diverse needs of the people and thereby fostering a more organic unity based on a wide dispersal of stakes in the system? The answer to this question depends on three things: one's view of the model of democracy that provides the basis of a national consensus in a multi regional, continental size, society; the presumed relationship between the model of democracy and the political process through which conflicts of interest and allegiance are mediated and resolved; and the expected relationship between the political process emanating from a given model of democracy and the performance of the system in economic and social spheres. The credibility of a democratic system, indeed the legitimacy of democracy as such, will depend on its capacity to deliver the goods. The question is: what can best ensure this? Concentrating vital decision-making in the apex of the system or operating from centers that are close to where the people are?

The case for centralization has been based on a series of arguments most of which happen to be specious. The most clever of these arguments, one that carries weight with many people (especially the intellectuals), is that the central government is more enlightened than the state governments and the state governments more so than local elected bodies which tend to be dominated by local vested interests and the upper castes. This is a clever argument because it smoothly tapers over the deeply entrenched interests and upper caste character of the elites at the higher levels, advances a progressive argument for perpetuating the status quo, and subtly condemns the vast rural hinterlands in which eighty percent of our people live into believing that their deliverance lies in surrendering their political rights to higher level elites. One is reminded of one's colonial past: you can either have self-government or good government, but not both. In the new setting the assumption is that only the Center can provide good government.

1. The Indian political system has been in a stagnant position for many years and now finds itself in a deadlock. Neither authoritarian nor the Westminister style parliamentary democratic approach seems to work. The main snag in both is the centralization of the political process, intended and deliberate in one, innate in the other. No restructuring along an alternative framework of development is possible without opening up the democratic structure and moving it closer to the base.

2. The existence of massive poverty has all these years been made an excuse for concentrating power and resources at the Centre, presumably because it could deal with it better. For some time, failure to do so was ascribed to local vested interests. Later, it was felt that the policies were not right and there was need for an alternative framework of policy. It is now clear that the biggest vested interest emanates from the nature of the Indian State and that no amount of tinkering with policy will change things. What needs to be changed is the nature of the State and the statist assumption that the problems of the people can be resolved through the machinery of the State.
3. This statistic assumption is in turn based on a fundamentally technological view of human problems. This is the view that deep-seated social maladies like pervasive poverty based on a system of deprivation can be removed by technological means only. We know that this is not true, that the removal of poverty and other deep-seated social maladies is an essentially political task, a task in which the people who are most affected participate in making the decisions that affect them. Building such a structure of participation is far more important for the removal of social and economic ills than are development programmes from above, no matter how well-conceived they are. Such a structure of participation is inherent in the democratic premise on which the Indian polity is supposed to be base. But the pre-existing State did not permit such a polity to evolve. It was

colonial State drawing its authority form the masters and not from the people. This State still survives, even if in an attenuated form. There is a new set of masters in command but many elements of colonial rule still persist and there does exist a measure of colonial relationship between New Delhi and lower down.

4. To move towards a structure of democratic participation of the type discussed here necessarily involves changing the structure of the State. This involves a change in power relationships between the Centre the States and lower down. Without such change, Indian democracy is bound to run into a deadlock and sooner or later flounder. The sway and power of charisma is linked in direct proportion to the lack of structure and institutionalization of the political process. Only a decentralized State can provide such institutional safeguards against the cult of personality and the role of Charisma. Everything seems to point to the need for decentralization. It is indeed an historic necessity.
5. Is it possible to move towards decentralization without providing greater autonomy and commensurate resources to the States? I do not think so. Merely holding elections of panchayats and municipalities does not mean decentralization. They need to have significant power and resources to work with and they need to be organized vertically through functional interrelationships along various tiers reaching out to the State level. This is not possible without first (or simultaneously) endowing the States themselves with significant power and resources.

6. There are two opposite temptations that the Centre and the States must respectively avoid. One is the temptation for national leaders to engage in a direct appeal to lower levels without permitting intermediate structures to grow; the modern version of this is populism. The other danger is in the opposite direction, namely, the growth of regional overlords through the increased power of the States which is not shared further down. To steer clear of both these dangers, it is essential to agree that greater autonomy for the States is at once part of a larger process of decentralization and an essential pre-requisite thereof.
7. Two other corollaries are necessary in the Indian case. First, there is nothing sacrosanct about autonomy at the level of existing State; in many of them there is need to provide autonomy to important regions within the State by slitting it. Second, there is a genuine fear that the more prosperous and powerful States will benefit more from the process of devolution. This should at all costs be avoided. Indeed, one of the justifications of greater autonomy at the State level is that it will put an end to the present situation in which advanced States get the better of the others by virtue of their pull at the Centre. The new strategy should be to both allow a large measure of self-reliance at the State level so that hitherto untapped potentials are released—this itself will begin to narrow disparities—and at the same time provide transitional correctives by weighted allocations and transfers.

8. Such corollaries only underline the ultimate aim of any democratic re-structuring: enabling the people to participate in shaping their collective future. Political decentralization is only a means to this and federalism a means to that means. Institutional structures by themselves produce no change, so much depends on the interest, the vigilance and the organization of the people themselves. But in the absence of an institutional structure that responds to people's initiatives, it is not possible to mount them. Indeed, the institutional innovations designed to respond to historic needs from time to time provide the stud of a dynamic polity. The difficulty with a functioning democracy is that it so much disarms the people that a revolutionary upheaval becomes impossible to mount. But the great thing about a functioning democracy is that it can itself become a vehicle of revolutionary change through structural changes in response to historic needs. And it can do this without an upheaval. But if it fails to do this for long, its future is in peril.

The problem of national integration is no longer political. It largely economic and demographic. It has two major dimensions: integration through removal of regional economic disparities most of which are to be found within existing states: and integration of rural and urban areas in the country which continue to be two different worlds. The problem of integration will henceforth need to be tackled in the context of forging viable organization forms along the federal system so that the accentuation of disparities along these two dissensions is minimized. While the basic issues are economic—both in terms of narrowing disparities and hence promoting justice and in terms of raising the general level of growth and productivity in the less development regions—their resolution calls for a political initiative.

To recapitulate my argument so far, there is really no doubt that without a large measure of decentralization, the problems facing this country will not be talked. These problems are primarily economic—creation of jobs and opportunities at the level where the people live and curbing inequalities that have arisen as a result of centralization of the planning process and undue concentration of economic power. But they are also political (in respect of correcting the highly distorted elite mass relationship), administrative (in respect of a restructuring of bureaucratic organization and a dispersal of administrate and technical talent to the districts) and educational (in respect of a return to the emphasis on primary education and literacy). If socialism is not once again to degenerate into a blousing bureaucracy which provided an elaborate structure of corruption, there is need to restrain the creation of ever new bodies at the center and instead, to enable the lower levels of the system to function effectively.

This is one point. It should at once be admitted, however, that there is economies confusion in the country on both the concepts of decentralization and the steps that are recommended to implement it. Advocates of these steps often talk as if there was no distinction between decentralization and fragmentation of the country into hundreds or thousands of self-governing communities—on some kind of a romanticized model of village republics based on a complete distortion of Gandhi is views on Swaraj. There is an opposite viewpoint advocated in the main by planners and growth men who think of decentralization in terms of creating organizational agencies at block and village levels who will carry out directives from above and mobilize local people to serve the ends set at higher levels.

Both these models are not only unsuited to the needs of this country; they also violate the basic tenets of a decentralized polity whose end is to create a democrat community in which the individual is the end and government a means to that end.

The first of the approach described above, which we may call the communitarian approach, confuses autonomy and self-reliance of individuals with the cohesion and unanimity of local communities. It confounds the need to share power for common ends with some kind of a compulsion to dismantle the state and the authority of the center. Its basic flaw lies in not perceiving that the concept of decentralization presupposes a center and everything that having a center in a political society involves—a common destiny as a people, consensus of fundamental values, and integrity. Decentralization is meaningful only in the context of such a sense of overall unity of purpose in which all individuals join at various levels of the socio-political system or, to use Gandhi's integral phraseology through a series of concentric circles that are ever widening, newer ascending.

The opposite approach to the fragmented communitarian one, which we may call the pyramidal approach confounds the need for self-reliance and self-government with agency functions in which not only is the individual made a cog in a vast machine but the machine itself begins to suffer from intense apoplexy at the center. It also fails to realize that the center in such a pyramid, under conditions of poverty and extent reliance for both economic and security reasons, tends to shift outside the country and that internal process of domination and exploitation are in fact part of a more global pattern of domination and exploitation.

The centralizing elite tends not only to delude the people over which it rules with all kinds of slogans and panaceas but also deludes itself that it is really setting the pace for the countries process towards democracy and socialism. In reality a centralized state violates both democracy and socialism it also undermines the principles of autonomy and self-reliance that we have come to value.

The task that faces us now is to make this autonomy that have acquired as a state, real for our people. In order do so, we will have to do a lot of thinking for ourselves, on a variety of choices, including on the kind of socialism that suits us and is in keeping with our values and traditions. For it is clear that none of the European brands including maims will suit our needs. All imported brands of socialism carry a large does of centralization and they have all undermined both man and nature in the process. We who value both the individuality of man and the inviolability of nature, must make our own choices in our economic model, in the technology that we adopt, in the nature of our state.

During the last four decades we have gone heavily in the direction of centralization—economically, technologically and even political, despite our federal democratic structure. Gandhi had warned us against these developments and advocated his model decentralization Nehru who was presiding over the phase of national integration and initiating a process of economic self-reliance both of which forced him to centralize the state, was nonetheless so heavily committed to the democratic ideal that he not only supported but took keen interest in the development of democratic decentralization in the country.

After Nehru there has been as sliding back on this process, thanks largely to the very considerable concentration of political authority in the hands of a few men of power presiding over huge party machines and patronage network. During that period local self-government suffered a sharp decline extent in two or three states and consequently whatever structure had been creator for undertaking programmers at the grassroots has been rendered weak and ineffective.

It now involves two major tasks-a restructuring of federal relations by establishing them on former footing and a reorientation of the process of economic planning and education with a view to ensuring the widest possible participation of the people in employment and output. Seen in this way, decentralization poses neither a fragmented view of the polity as found in the communitarian approach nor a mere proliferation of centrally controlled structures at lower levels as implied in the pyramidal approach. Rather, decentralization is to conceived as a step in the direction of a more integrated polity, a better performing economy and a model of social reconstruction necessary for a properly functioning democracy and a genuinely socialist state (the one necessarily involves the other).

Decentralization in the present context entails the above steps. Indeed, it provides the basic and necessary structural dimension of that package. The bland formulation of both the communication and the pyramidal approaches must give place to a more integral view of decentralization. Gandhi's view of decentralization was precisely such. Since his days decentralization has acquired an almost obscurantist connotation, thanks largely to the vulgar gentians.

Hence the great promise of the various experiments in decentralizing power to the people. For it is the only way of ensuring radical change through the democratic process and not in violation of it. Instead of conceiving Panchayati Raj, i.e. of people's power. The earlier concept grew out of the failure of the community development administration in involving the people in the development process and hence, following the Balwantrai Mehta Committee report, the thought of Panchayati Raj institutions for the same. People were to be made into efficient instruments of development, instead of viewing development as an instrument of the people. That report was an essential step in the direction of debureaucratizing development. Today we need to go beyond it.

The tern people power can of course, be misleading as the useful question is which people? There is no necessary correlation between institutional decentraliaztion and decentralization in class terms. Such correlation can never be legislated straight away except through entitlements over schemes, ecology and assets like land. Some of this has been provided in some legislations (e.g. Karnataka) through transfer of a large measure of resources and functions and of rights of ownership and control vested in manual Panchayati and Zilla Parishads. But we have by now enough experience to suggest that far more crucial than legally laid out control and access is the mobilization of men and women committed to a genuinely radical democratic transformation. We have to wait and see whether this in fact takes place.

The useful divide (and often hostility) between party and non-party active and between state and society, is less pronounces in settings that are so small and in what ultimately matters is sustained and dedicated work.

Much will depend on how political parties committed to democratic opportunities opening up at lower levels of the polity are able to at once begin a process of party-building from the grassroots upwards (instead of the top down approach of setting up ad-hoc committees) and transcend narrow party interests and think of the people instead. By the same token the various activists groups need to grap the full significance of the new opportunities, to avail of them in full earnestness and to forge ahead with a give place to the only polarity that has come to the fore in recent years-between the people and the elite, between the democratic spirit and the bureaucratic straight jacket, between mafia politics and the much talked of value–based political life.

A crucial challenge faces Indian democracy today. It is necessary that the issue is not left merely in hands of governments and parties, prisoners of entrenched interests and narrow time-spans. It is an issue on which non-party actives, intellectuals opinion-makers and the concerned citizenry as a whole should keep the pressure on.

Panchayati Raj is too important to be left to governments and parties. It much be seen as part of the political process that emanates from the grassroots.

Employment Crying for Panchayat Raj

It is no rhetoric to say that the strategy of full employment cannot be worked on the ground without Panchayati Raj institutions. Every social idea requires an appropriate institution to deliver its promise. It applies even more so to the realization of the goal of full employment in our conditions.

What are our conditions? An understanding of our situation is pivotal to both the formulation of an appropriate strategy of full employment as well as to the designing of appropriate institutional mechanisms for operationalising the strategy of full employment.

We may draw here from an excellent review of the trends of employment/unemployment from a working paper by Dr. T.S. Papola prepared for the Planning Commission. This paper points out that while the economy has been crying for employment, the rate of growth of employment has, in fact, been falling over the years. It was 2.82 percent during 1973-78, 2.22 percent during 1978-83 and is estimated to have been 1.55 percent during 1983 to 1987-88. This decline over the years in the rate of growth is noticed in all components of the workforce and in all sectors except Mining and Construction. In agriculture, employment as grown at less than 1 percent per annum, and in services, manufacturing and transport at 2.5 percent, 2 percent and 2.7 percent annum, respectively, during 1983-88 (table 1).

Another aspect of trends in employment which should be a matter of concern to all those engaged in rural development in particular, is the fact that rural employment in the period 1972-73 to 1977-78 has grown at a rate of only 1.75 percent annum which is below the national average of 2 percent per annum and drastically below the 4 percent growth of urban employment in the corresponding period (Table 2). Increasing suffocation of employment opportunities in the rural areas is driving large numbers to seek livelihood in the urban areas where conditions of life relating to housing, sanitation are nothing short of stinking sums.

Table 1: Growth of Employment* by Major Sectors 1973-88

Sector	*1972-73 to 1977-78*	*1977-78 to 1983*	*1983 to 1987-88*	*1972-73 to 1987-88*
Agriculture	2.32	1.20	0.65	1.37
Mining	4.68	5.85	6.16	5.47
Manufacturing	5.10	3.75	2.10	3.61
Construction	1.59	7.45	13.69	7.23
Elect. Gas & Water supply	12.23	5.07	4.64	7.06
Communication, Transport & Storage	4.85	6.35	2.67	4.65
Services	3.67	4.69	2.50	3.05
Total	2.82	2.22	1.55	2.17

* Usual Principal and Subsidiary Status.

Table 2: Growth Rates of Employment* by Sex and Residence

Sex / Residence	*1972-73 to 1977-78*	*1977-78 to 1983*	*1983 to 1987-88*	*1972-73 to 1987-88*
Rural	2.52	1.74	0.95	1.75
Urban	4.31	4.10	3.79	4.00
Male	2.61	2.15	1.81	2.19
Female	3.23	2.36	1.04	2.24
Total	2.82	2.22	1.55	2.21

*Usual Principal and Subsidiary Status.

Papola also points out that the organized sector which is regarded by many as the engine of growth has been particularly incapable of delivering employment to the economy –whatever else it may deliver by way of goods and services.

Deceleration in the rate of employment growth has been even sharper in the recent years in the organized sector. While the long term rate of growth of organized sector employment has been around 2 percent per annum, it has declined from 2.42 percent during 1978-83 to 1.36 percent during 1983-87 (table 3). The deceleration is observed generally in all sectors, but it has been steepest in manufacturing which accounts for roughly one-fourth of organized sector employment.

Table 3: Deceleration in the Rate of Employment Growth

Sector	1972-73	1977-78	1983-1987	1973-1987
Agriculture	2.40	1.07	1.50	1.63
Mining	5.47	2.65	0.17	2.78
Manufacturing	2.42	1.74	0.06	1.44
Construction	3.04	3.50	3.29	3.35
Elect. Gas & Water supply	(-)2.06	1.72	1.34	0.37
Communication, Transport & storage	1.70	2.16	1.12	1.70
Services	3.04	3.07	2.11	2.77
Total	2.48	2.42	1.36	2.11

Another worrisome feature of the trends in employment is a major shift in the structure of workforce. There is an increase in the proportion of casual labour relative to the self–employed and regular salaried wage workers. For rural and urban areas taken together, over the fifteen year period, from 1972-73 to

1987–88, there was an increase in casual wage labour from 23 to 30 percent with a steady decline in self–employment from 61 to 56 percent. Within these overall trends, there are some differences between the rural and urban areas. Increase in the proportion of casual wage labour has been accompanied by a decline in the proportion of the self–employed in rural areas. In urban areas, it appears to have been caused by a decline in the proportion of regular wage/salaried workers. The pace of casualisation is found to be faster in the case of male than of female workers, though the proportion of casual wage labour has uniformly been higher among female than among male workers.

Further, unorganized sector accounts for about 90 percent of the total employment and its share has been more or less constant throughout the fifteen year period. Though the shares of organized and unnorganised sector in total employment have not changed over the years, there have been significant increases in the proportion of the unorganized sector in some sectors of economic activity. In manufacturing, the share of the unorganized sector in total employment has increased from 67 percent in 1972-73 to 76 percent in 1987-88. Unorganised sector now accounts for about 86 percent of the employment in construction. In transport, storage and communication, the proportion has gone up from 24 –51 percent during this period.

An increase in employment at an average rate of two percent per annum during the Seventies and the Eighties has not been found to be high enough to take care of the backlog and the addition to the labour force. In 1972-73, the backlog of unemployment was estimated to be around 8 million. Labour force was estimated to be growing at a rate of 2.5 percent per annum. Labour force participation rates have registered a marginal decline over the years, and therefore, growth in labour force during the Eighties is estimated to be around 2.2 percent per annum. But as observed earlier, the rate of employment growth has also decelerated during recent years. As a result, the backlog of unemployment has been rising. On the basis of data available from 43rd round of NSS (1987-88), unemployment was estimated to be 12.43 million according to Usual principal Status (UPS), 15.30 million according to Weekly Status (WS) and 18.95 million (person years) according to Daily Status (DS) (Table 4).

Table 4

Worker	*Year*	*Rural*			*Urban*			*Total*
		Male	*Female*	*Total*	*Male*	*Female*	*Total*	*(R+U)*
UPS	1983	2.12	1.41	1.91	5.86	6.90	6.04	2.77
	1987-88	2.87	3.52	3.07	6.07	8.77	6.56	3.77
WS	1983	3.72	4.26	3.88	6.69	7.46	6.81	4.51
	1987-88	4.16	4.27	4.19	6.71	8.93	7.12	4.80
DS	1983	7.52	8.98	7.94	9.23	10.99	9.52	8.25
	1987-88	4.58	6.91	5.25	8.79	12.00	9.26	6.09

UPS – Usual Principal Status. Person is considered unemployed according to this concept if he/she was available for but without work for a major part of the year.

WS - Weekly Status. A person is considered unemployed according to this concept if he/she, though being available for work did not have work even one hour during the reference week.

Not only the absolute magnitude of unemployment has been increasing over the year; but the open unemployment rates have also been rising in recent years. Unemployment rates according to UPS criterion increased from 2.77 percent in 1983 to 3.77 percent in 1987-88 and according to WS from 4.51 percent to 4.80 percent. Besides, the structure of unemployment seems to be shifting from the predominance of underemployment towards rise in open unemployment.

Within the broad trend towards an increasingly open chronic character of unemployment, the following features may be considered of special significance. One, this trend is seen to be particularly strong in case of rural areas, where the usual status unemployment has increased from 1.91 percent of labour force in 1983 to 3.07 percent in 1987-88, and daily status unemployment has declaimed from 7.94 percent to 5.25 percent Second, the trend in the increase in the incidence of open unemployment was stronger in the case of women than of men. Third, the differences between the usual status and daily status unemployment rates are much larger in the case of women than in the case of men, which implies that underemployment is a much higher proportion of overall unemployment in the case of women than of men.

Incidentally, five States, viz. Tamil Nadu, Andhra Pradesh, Kerala, West Bengal and Uttar Pradesh account for 56 per cent of the total unemployed person days.

None the less, a crucial aspect of our unemployment is under employment, i.e. there are over 230 million persons who have partial work or work for part of the year. How to fill the blanks? This means that additional work opportunities should be such as to supplement their present work income profile until we have massive new opportunities to ensure full time work for them in some new vocations. This also implies that, until then, they cannot be uprooted from their location which is providing them partial work today.

The deceleration in the growth rate of employment assumes threatening dimensions when seen in the context of relentless demographic pressures in India. According to the Census of 1991, the population of India in absolute terms has increased nearly by 161 million during the '80s. It is projected that by the end of the century, there will be an addition of equal number s to our population taking the total number over 1,000 million mark.

Keral is the lone shining example where demographic pressure has been contained and the infant mortality rate too brought down to 23 compared with the national average of 94. Studies have shown that spatially widespread and effective delivery of elementary education and primary health services are two major identifiable factors underlying Kerala's success in curbing the population growth rate But this lesson is not imbibed by any other state. Though the combine expenditure of the states during the 80s on primary health ad primary education was a staggering Rs.65,000 crore, most of the school teachers do not tech and the health workers do not treat, "we are not your servants" is the commonly heard answer given by thee functions when questioned by the village population as to why should they draw their salaries if they do not carry out their duties.

Thus, despite huge expenditure, the population growth rate continues unabated, ad vast segments of the rural population remain illiterate, and their health uncared for. Only in Karnataka, where these functionaries were brought under the control of the mandal Panchayats, did they perform their duties.

Recent economic reforms are daring, if not dynamic—but from a certain point of view. First the reform package does not even address itself to measures for effective delivery and spread of primary education and health that can help to contain the demographic pressure as in Kerala. Second, the thrust of reforms, such as they are, is to transfer much of the initiative for development and the pattern of growth of the economy to the market. If the past experience is any guide, the organnised sector of industry is steadily pushing down the rate of labour absorption per unit of capital or output, as noted earlier. Remember , much of this phenomenon of declining labout absorption in the past fifteen years occurred during the period of rigorous industrial regulation and control over investment, choice of technology and choice of location. If those regulatory instruments could not prevent the steady fall in the rate of employment in organized industry, then it is axiomatic that left to the market forces the choice of techniques/products would be even more pronouncedly anti-labour-absorption per unit of capital and output than in the past.

Then there is the awesome pressure of deficits and debts, which raises doubts whether we have the resources in the first place to obtain full employment conditions. Unfortunately, the term 'resources' has come to be identified almost wholly with financial resources and that too budgetary resources.

Today, the budget is practically bankrupt form the development view point. It is no longer able to generate a surplus for investment on development. It cannot meet even current revenue expenditure. The deicit is increasingly being met through public debt. The latter has now increased to intolerable proportions. The consequent burden of interest charges has emerged as the single largest item in the budget overtaking even the dreaded Defence expenditure. Therefore, even if we were inclined to continue to rely on financial/ budgetary resources fro investment on development—the option is no longer open to us. But is not true that we have run dry of all resources. The most massive and one might say, fabulous resources available to us for development purposes have yet to be harnessed fully or property. For example sol, water, vegetation. Their potential for productivity increases as well as additional employment is admitted as being enormous. But they have suffered from neglect. Indeed, if anything, lot of wanton damage has been inflicted upon these resources at the altar of organized industry and infrastructure. This is not the opinion of street agitators waving the environmental flag—but that of the ministry of Environment.

Besides, in terms of resources for development, we have today a huge network of technical , social, scientific institutions in the country whose resources remain untapped for development. Further, we have the vast power of the scientific instrument of remote sensing. The Natural resources Data Management System (NRDMS) of the Department of Science and Technology as well as the Space Department have developed sufficient skill and resources in mapping the ground resources of soil, water, vegetation and minerals—which can totally transform the character of our development planning and endeavour. But planning of use of natural resources or their conservation/regeneration has to be area based. That in turn is diametrically opposite of sectoral planning that we have almost exclusively relied on hitherto. Sectoral planning without the framework of area planning is fragmentary and often disjointed.

Practically in our set-up where sectoral departments are not on talking terms with each other, the disjointedness is destructive of scarce resources. An elementary need of efficiency is the mutually reinforcing impact of different sectoral investments. Efforts. But alas, the pattern of our development administration, i.e., its sectoral compartmentalization is the arch enemy of this elementary principle of efficient use of resources. Bureaucratic rigidities which frustrate area planning (as attempted on experimental basis in water shed development projects) are only one of the villains. More important of the villains is the lack of local institutions without which area planning cannot even be conceived of. And since area planning will have to order local priorities. Mobilize local resources and optimize on existing investment—it has to be backed by the people or rather it has to rest on the shoulders of the people and led by them. It cannot be a bureaucratic venture.

People-led development would mean not only so many shoulders—but more so their stake in development, their idealism, ideas, imagination as well as some material resources too—all of which are denied today to our development endeavour.

This is where Panchayati Raj enters the scene. In the event, it is not only a measure of democratic decentralization but also one of downright rationalization.

If we are able to optimize on existing resources, broaden our base of resources for development and provide for an area–based local institution in every nook and corner of the country, to plan and implement through men and women who have the highest stake in local progress a full-scale war on unemployment can be well and truly launched and sustained.

The magnitude of the task of full employment and the complexity of strategy necessary is mind–boggling. At the beginning of the year 1990-91, about 16 million persons, 10 million in rural areas and 6 million in urban areas, are estimated to be unemployed (on weekly status basis). Of these 12 million are males and 4 million females. Another 12 million are estimated as severely underemployed. Thus the backlog of unemployment could be taken to be around 28 million (Table 5).

Table 5: Estimates of Unemployment as on April 1,1990

		Male	*Female*	*Total*
I	By usual Status (UPS)			
	Rural	4.97	2.66	7.63
	Urban	4.16	1.30	5.46
	Total	9.13	3.96	13.09
II	By usual weekly Status (CWS)			
	Rural	7.06	2.92	9.98
	Urban	4.59	1.31	5.90
	Total	11.65	4.23	15.88
III	By Current Daily Status (CDS)/Equivalent million person years			
	Rural	7.75	4.59	12.34
	Urban	5.91	1.66	7.57
	Total	13.66	6.25	19.90

Note: These figures relate to the population in age group5.

Source: All the five Tables are from the Publication Employment Past Trends and Prospects for 1990s – Working Paper": Planning Commission, New Delhi, May 1990.

Laour force is projected to grow by 37 million during 1990-95 and another 41million during 1995-2000, Employment would have to grow to a rate of over 4 percent per annum to reach the goal of near full employment by 1995 and over 3 percent per annum if it is to be reached by 2000. Given the past trends and prospects in the near future, it would only be realistic to aim at this goal by 2000.

The goal would only be fesible if employment is consciously built into the development strategy, so that the growth is mainly derived from the sectors and sub-sectors with high employment intensity. On the basis of an analysis of the recent trends, the following would constitute the major elements of such a strategy.

(i) A rapid and geographically diversified growth of agriculture so that the hitherto lagging regions have a major share in agricultural growth during the 1990's:

(ii) Diversification of agriculture into non-staple high value crops, particularly in the areas of relatively developed agriculture; and

(iii) Development of an appropriate support and policy framework for the growth of non-agricultural , particularly manufacturing, activities in rural areas, including rural towns.

The setting up of area-based panchayats will not necessarily make the delivery of full employment a painless task. There will be many a sleepless night, but without the creation of this basic institutional infrastructure lively with lakhs of elected men and women representatives to man it, the goal of full employment will remain a distant dream.

3

Panchayati Raj, Development and Developmental Performance: An Institution Building Perspective

Panchayati Raj, being level of government (local) has an administrative component. A good number of persons, used to a narrower focus on administration, or bureaucracy, and its assumed 'non–political' character tend to emphasise the instrumental (administrative) character of Panchayati Raj. However, social scientists, and a large number of others better attended to nuanced thinking, have be gone beyond this focus. Them, the appeal of, and resistance to, Panchayati Raj has a political dimension. In this perspective, the view about its instrumental character is itself political. The concept of politics is subtler than ordinarily supposed.

Politics involves us all, for all of us are involved in structured relations (associated with all institutions, orgnisations and their sub-sets, and not merely governmental ones). Views or ideologies of values systems informing such relations, and activities and process impinging upon their continuance or change, are all political. The popular notion of politics as pursuit of personal or group aggrandizement through unscrupulous means, is hopelessly inadequate. If one were to be guided by it, movements for national emancipation, social reform or revolution, or their ancillary manifestations, would not be political. These movements, or struggles, have often brought forth the noblest urges of human nature. That, in modern times, they have been mediated in varying degrees by the State is not the only ground of their political character In the view explained above, such struggles would be so even otherwise (The politics of gender discrimination, of appropriate technology, of greening and so on, could be cited as example). For greater lucidity, a more helpful way of understanding the point would be a sharper focus on power structure, irrespective of its remoteness from the state. The subtler dimension is the normative order sustaining structured relations with the tangible aspect reflected in who gets what, how and why? In terms of status, prestige and material advantage. Practically all over the world, the basic values of the modern civilization—human dignity, freedom, equality and justice—have conditioned perceptions and evaluations of a given normative order in the context of the dynamics of change.

To the extent development entails this dynamics, its gut meanings would be political. The political character of Panchayati Raj derives from the following considerations: *(i)* a level of government, it is an integral part of the state structure, *(ii)* political processes, involving political parties, link up center, state and locality various ways, *(iii)* the gut political meanings of development shape its legislative and operational content, and *(iv)* rural society, with a higher salience of traditionality (rigours of caste hierarchy, etc.) might set a stronger political agenda for Panchayati Raj could be visualized as a vital çomponent of the societal direction systems, and therefore, as a strategic vehicle of development. And if one takes the view that the level of backwardness of rural India, and the developmental gap between it (Bharat) and urban India (India) is politically unacceptable, the accent on the political content of rural development, and on the contribution of Panchayati Raj, would be sharper. It follows that any view, review or redefinition of policies and implementation strategies relating to rural development is not a politically neutral proposition.

Rural development with or without Panchayti Raj would, thus, represent two different political scenarios, depending partly upon the why the centrality of economic growth is viewed in the scheme of development, whatever the standpoint, Panchayati Raj is bound to impinges on the meaning and content of developmental performance. The real issue is not whether it des but whether its results would be negative, positive or, more likely, a mix of both.

Hypothetically, there could be many sets of answers. Bu t the evolving universals—liberal democratic ideology and a model of economic growth where the GNP is not the sole deity—reduce the alternatives to a broad set where nuances rather than irreconcilable differences define the idiom of discourse. We hasten to add that without a close attention to contextual (country specific) details, the answers would lack operational relevance. Within this broad framework, we attempt a discussion of the contribution of Panchayati Raj vis-a-vis the following issues:

1. Whether economic growth is posited on certain political conditions, and if so what could be the complexion of these conditions if economic development is significantly titled towards equity and distributive justice?
2. What is the relevance of liberal principles to district level administration, and below?
3. Could the concept of overhead democracy be considered tenable?
4. Even if the case for Panchayati Raj is conceded in principle what have been the negative features of its functioning so far, and what can be done about them.
5. Despite the malfunctioning of Panchayati Raj in some respects, can it make any concrete contribution to economic growth?
6. Can district administration be made more responsive or its performance be made more effective, without Panchayati Raj and what is the bearing of such administration on economic growth?
7. Does the trend towards sustainable development warrant a fresh look at the case for decentralized development?
8. Are the stronger decentralist trends in evidence in large parts of the west in any way relevant to conditions in India.
9. What improvements, if any, are needed in the present politico administrative climate to make it conducive to the evolution of Panchayati Raj on sounder lines?

If it is contended that the issues themselves have a political bias, we might as well plead guilty, on the premise that all such issues are inevitably so. Much, however, depends upon the tenor and quality of the analysis, and should it turn out to be good in terms of content, those with a case against Panchayati Raj should be able to benefit by it. And counterpoints emerging from the attack could help chisel or reorient the issues, and so on. It is hoped that our discussion would enlarge the area of shared rational ground., and hopefully render theological acerbities at the extremities less plausible.

We tackle the issues in the sequence in which they appear above:

1. Among the basic political conditions necessary for economic growth of any type, law and order, and an environment of peace, a political ecology, conducive to a relatively more stable and efficient pursuit of the ordinary business' of life, would get priority. Dictatorial, or strong bureaucratic, regimes might well register short-term successes in ensuring such an environment. But certain inherent brittleness makes the regimes highly vulnerable. The tension generating-and-resolving democratic regimes are likely to be on a wide canvas, more tensile and less vulnerable. In any case, India with democratic polity of a sturdier variety in the region is region, is bound to be closer to the tensile model with democratic legitimacy determining the contours o n evolving stability posited on a pragmatic management of potential or actual tremors through legitimacy building statesmanship. This is not possible without some minimal attention to the urge for participation ad equity among hitherto excluded segments. In India, because of the caste system and high levels of poverty, such segments are bound to

pose a formidable problem both quantitatively and qualitatively. The legitimacy building process is thus bound to have a more poignant meaning for them, particularly in rural areas where more than 70 percent of the population still resides. Acuter levels of poverty and socio-cultural backwardness here make the picture more somber, In such a setting, the contribution of Panchayati Raj to legitimacy building cannot be gainsaid, even if it is contended that its impact on the process of economic growth may not be all that smooth. Here is a developmental dilemma. Economic growth would gain through conducive political ecology because of Panchayati Raj; it might suffer if the ecology is not conducive. Events have an element of unpredictability about them. The impact of negative features can perhaps be reduced. When reduced, the trade-off would be better, if there is an irreducible minimum, one has to come to terms with two wise maximal because human nature is imperfect human institution are bound to be imperfect (Swami Yatiswarnanda); and if a thing has a positive side, it will have a negative side too'. Nothing is an unmixed blessing. Pnachayati Raj, therefore, like every human institution would yield results which are not just positive or negative, but a mix of both. The real issue, then, is whether the mix of positive, and negative aspects of the performance of Panchayati Raj in relation to the interaction between political ecology and economic growth has more of the former than the latter. A categorical yes would have been easier in an intellectual climate characterized by a strong belief in the plasticity of human nature and admitting no limits on human perfectibility. Despite a reassuring Third Wave Civilization' scenario in vogue among some futurologists, social scientists these days tend to be more hard-headed. The human world is likened to a 'garbage can' it can be cleansed to a large extent, but a residue of garbage cannot be eliminated. We have to live with it, while striving all the time to explore the potential for improvement and to devise the organizational and technological means for achieving it. Even then, the reach of the successive outer circles of developmental ripples would be much wider than is ordinarily supposed. In other words, while one must not ignore realities, one must not ignore possibilities either. Those with conservative inclinations tend to underplay the latter, and vice versa. Depending upon one's standpoint, one might be involved in the politics of developmental pessimism or optimism. Panchayati Raj can be assailed by some on grounds of realism; but realism, more often than not could be a convenient clock for camouflaging the vested interests of higher level political elites and bureaucracy, and of the wider configurations of associated power structures. As the character of development and the dynamics of legitimacy building cannot be viewed in isolation, and as Panchayati Raj has implications for both, postures of political neutrality should be treated with caution. A conservative person might prefer a kind of legitimacy building which does not go beyond the requirements of stability; but this has to contend with other approaches to development, depending upon the character and strength of other socio-political forces. Conservative resistance, notably manifested in the bureaucratic segment, is a factor in the balance of forces. To the extent this is countered by forces on the other side of the barricade, as it were, stability has to be viewed in the wider political terms of legitimacy building discussed earlier, rather than an unilinear view of economic growth. Social reality involves complex complementaries, and we should,

Social reality involves complex complementaries, and we should, therefore, think of trade–offs rather than discrete categories in which economic growth is put in a compartment as though it has nothing to do with political development. Recent trends in economic thought, infact, underline a more direct bearing of the political dimension (understood in the sense explained earlier) on economic growth. In his book, The Nature of Mass Poverty, Galbraith makes the following points on the theme of mass poverty, as distinct from 'case' poverty, in countries like India. It is rural poverty... that is intractable; it is the equilibrium of rural poverty which evokes... circular causation; the poverty of the poor country denies its people the means for improvement, and when they become available there are built into the structure of poverty the social and biological forces by which improvement is aborted, the poverty perpetuated; and there is a world of difference between the poor and rich countries—in one case, an equilibrium of poverty and, in the other, the protected dynamic of change. The more important differences in acculturation—in accommodation to the culture of poverty. More than the factors usually mentioned (Selected more for their convenience than for their validity)—natural resource endowment; nature of the government, and the economic, educational, and administrative systems; capital and technology—it is accommodation which touches the heart of mass poverty. Rejection of accommodation, resulting in a more effective aggregation of the energy and thrust for accomplishment, is a basic condition for removing mass poverty, and for economic growth. The difference—the vital and largely unexplored difference between different poor countries lies in the number of their citizens who refuse accommodation and who seek escape from the equilibrium of poverty either within the community or by leaving it. Now, rejection of, or countering accommodation, is a political proposition a matter of, what Ripon had said in the context of his reforms in local self-government more than a century ago, political and popular education. To this mild terminology, a modern student of political sociology would add process like conscientisation, empowerment, political mobilization, etc. These processes are largely explicatory in character, with political and popular education enriched in their core meaning vis-à-vis 'rejection' and 'countering' of accommodation. Many civil servants in India, better attuned to centralization and 'chain of command' rooted in colonial-feudal ethos, dislike the processes countering 'accommodation', on the ground of their being 'political'!.. If probed further, they would congratulate themselves on their capacity for being politically neutral, blissfully indifferent to the incongruence of their systemic ethos with the political ambience of the Constitution. Some of them are among those who favour a model of economic growth 'free' from politics. Leading development economists think otherwise. To Albert Hirschmand, economic performance 'depends not so much on funding optimal combination for given resources as on calling forth and enlisting..., resources and abilities that are hidden, scattered, or badly utilised'. In a trenchant critique of development economics as it had been practiced till then, he wrote: "In a Freudian act of displacement they 'took out' their distress over the political side on the weaker aspects of economic record". He admonished the conventional development economists for expecting the underdeveloped countries, with their over whelming problem of poverty', to perform like "wind-up" toys, and for perceiving them as having 'only interests and no passion. The sarcasm implied in the imagery of wind-up' toys would be apposite to Galbraith's (politics of) countering accommodation. The trickle–down mechanism having failed to tackle the problem of poverty, leading economists have turned to the politics of 'basic needs' and human resource development, to remedy environmental deficiencies marked by social values and institutions that create poverty ingrained behaviour patterns and allow a stacking of the 'rules of the game' against lower classes. Amartya Sen, another renowned economist, shifts the focus of his analysis sharply towards 'entitlements', which, visualized as a person's or household's actual command over goods and services, depend upon 'political arrangement s (including pressure groups and news distribution systems)'. `The process of development', to him. 'is not primarily one of expanding the supply of goods and services but of enhancing the capabilities of people'. And capabilities are a function of entitlements. The gut issues in 'development', thus, are political, not only in the sense of political roots of economic growth, but also in the sense of a [referred political content of development. As Denis Goulet put it, Development always implies some vision of the good life, and the choice of preferred means for moving towards it. Economists with pretensions to a politically 'neutral' or `sterilized' approach, tend to support a model of economic growth ('savings and investment') notably on the decline; a good deal of technical sophistication often conceals a clever design to continue the tilt of the 'rules of the game' against the poor. For them the ringing declaration of Ignancy Sachs should serve as a curtain raiser: "The crisis of development is also a crisis of development theory. Economic growth alone, however rapid, cannot solve social problems and banish misery and unemployment. In the new political economy of development, the key concepts are: Equity, social satisfaction and basic needs. In the context of rigidly stratified and basic needs. In the context of rigidly stratified societies like that of India, these concepts acquire the character of imperative. Gunnar Myrdal reminded us long ago how subnormal nutritional and health standards affected productivity levels adversely. If we add to this the urges for participative development, more visible now everywhere, the case for a politically more egalitarian model of development becomes evident. In such a model, the contribution, of Panchayati Raj to weakening the culture of accommodation; to the empowerment of the ordinary people and to improving their entitlements; to unlimbering the rigider moulds of stratification through shuffling of elites and changes in power structure; to increasing the levels of social satisfaction and to meeting participatory urges—-and thereby, cumulatively to the processes of economic growth—can be confidently visualized on the basis of its demonstrated potential. This is the complex of political conditions on which economic growth is posited, with a significant tilt towards equity and distributive justice defining the contours of development' (a wider concept) to which the narrower pursuit of economic growth should be subordinated, partly for the reason that spin-offs of such a model of development for economic growth of even a conventional variety are not inconsiderable. A more obvious spin-off would be gains in administrative effectiveness. This us to the 'politics' administrative reforms, and to subsequent points.

2. In the earlier decades of the nineteenth century, Raja Ram Mohan Roy, the father of the Indian Renaissance, advocated the 'liberal principles of politics and religion' with conviction and courage. It was left to a British Viceroy to attempt an articulate exposition and application of liberal principles to the administrative sphere –where it (As the cutting–edge) mattered more: the district administration. As early as 1882 (Ripon's Resolution), he hit the bull's eye by describing the district administration as 'autocratic', a description which touched a raw nerve in the bureaucratic apparatus, for it carried an inconvenient political message. Perhaps a little too frank for its peripheral (feudal-cum-colonial) ethos. The agenda of administrative reforms, entailing the resolve to 'supersede' the existing 'more autocratic system' (of managing many branches of local affairs solely through the 'government district officers') was based on the following liberal principles (underlying the new scheme of local self-government).

i. 'It is not, primarily, with a view to improvement in administration that this measure is put forward and supported. It is chiefly desirable as an instrument of political and popular education.

ii. With the supersession of the 'more autocratic system', the Government officers were called upon to 'realise' that for them the new system opened a 'fairer field for the exercise of administrative tack and directive energy'.

iii. The government officers were expected to 'accept loyally and as their own the policy of the Government' to foster sedulously the small beginnings of `independent political life' in the management of the specified 'branches of local affairs.

iv. In a tone remarkably similar to that of Galbraith, the Resolution referred to the fact that 'the people of India are...remarkably tolerant of existing facts', and with a political passion born of the desire to set things right in the direction of the above principles, asserted that the Governor-General in Council does not attach much value to the 'theory' that the people of this country are themselves entirely indifferent to the principle of self-government; that they take but little interest in public matters; and that they prefer to have such affairs managed for them by government officers.

The enunciation of these principles was not merely an expression of political testament; it was also informed by pragmatism. Lord Ripon shrewdly observed that he 'himself has no doubt that, in course of time, as local knowledge and local interest are brought to bear ore freely upon local administration, improved efficiency ill, in fact, follow'. He had no doubt that there were bound to be 'many failures' in the beginning, 'calculated' 'in some cases to cast apparent discredit upon the practice of self–government itself'. The Resolution sought to reduce them through a subtle combination of tact and firmness vis-à-vis bureaucracy, In paragraph 7, an important reason for at least some of the failures was alluded to: that the principle (of local self-government) has not yet been, in any general or satisfactory sense, fully or fairly tried. There is reason to fear that previous attempts at local self-government have been too often over-ridden and practically crushed by direct, though well meant, official interference'. Should, in spite of a supportive official orientation, a 'period of failures' become inevitable, narrower considerations of administrative efficiency should be subordinated to the principles enunciated earlier. Without being oblivious of other pragmatic considerations, and in a sense to dispel misgivings (with gut political meanings) on that account, the Governor-General in council thought it necessary to state his conviction about the administrative and political imperatives behind his plan.

For a nineteenth century statesman (that too, one representing an imperial regime), this was a remarkably clear, and prescient, exposition of the relevance of liberal principles to the district and sub-district levels of administration. He following propositions explicate, amplify and update the above principles.

i. Swaraj is to be obtained by educating the masses to a sense of their capacity to regulate and control authority. When Panchayat Raj is established, public opinion will do what violence can never do. The present power of the Zamindars, the capitalists and the rajas can hold sway so long as the common people do not realize their own strength.

- *Mahatma Gandhi*

ii. 'Now (after 1947) the distinction between the rulers and the ruled has been removed. Nevertheless sometimes our officers consider themselves to be master. This (Panchayati Raj) is the real Swaraj of the people. Even as we put our faith in our people, so will they respond and help in building up this great country of ours.

- *Jawaharlal Nehru*

iii. 'The liberal ideology of local government endows it with two major functions in society : to serve the democratic objectives of participation, education, discussion and consent; and to provide services under such political direction in an efficient manner. The study of bureaucracy is a study of political power... bureaucratic structure of authority and bureaucratic power in the modern states create political costs for some sections of society and political benefits to others. The very structure of bureaucratic organsiation is in egalitarian.

iv. Although civil servants have direct technical responsibility for implementing programs of change, political factors and political agents play and important part in stimulating growth and accelerating development. Moderate conflict among politicians makes them bid for supporters by securing the latter goods and services from state sources. Such bids necessarily produce conflict between the change agents, as leaders exert pressure on administrators to release, or withhold, the desirable resources available in programs of state-stimulated development. But development programs get implemented faster and with better results'. Referring to the tendency to use the prevalence of conflict as an 'excuse the author observes as follows: 'I would argue, then that Panchayati Raj, the cooperative Movement, and other rural development Schemes have not atrophied because of the conflict inherent within them. These enunciations are illustrative rather than exhaustive. The first two have the added advantage of being articulated by the two greatest Indian political leaders of this century, and 'makers' of history. None of them would contend that the process of development mediated by local self government is conflict or tension free. These and other costs, however, are more than balanced by the gains associated with liberal political order spanning all the territorial levels from the 'locality' to the nation. This point has an integral connection with the next issue (overhead democracy) representing a nuance rather than a distinct entity.

3. A large number of civil servants, and a good many political leaders, suggest that democracy at the national (in a federal set-up at the 'state' level also) should be considered sufficient. After all, are not the political executives and legislators at these higher levels elected functionaries, accountable to the people of the large territorial units, and to an extent their small constituencies? Exponents of Panchayati Raj consider such a concept of 'overhead democracy inadequate. The following formulations illustrate their position.

i. 'Democracy is nothing unless it means in the last resort letting the people have their own way, not only in the mass , by means of an aggregate vote on a nation-wide scale, but also in their lesser groups and societies of which the great society is made up, and through which it is made articulate in such a way that the less clamorous voices can be heard.

- *G.D.H. Cole*

ii. 'Inhabitants of any given area have a consciousness of common purpose, a sense of the needs of their neighborhood, which only they can fully know. They find that the power to satisfy them of themselves gives to them a quality of vigour far greater in the happiness it produces than would be the case if satisfaction were always provided by, or controlled from without. For administration from without always lacks the vitalizing ability to be responsive to local opinion: it misses shades and expressions of thought and wants which are urgent to successful government.

- *Harold Laski*

iii. Our government jurisdictions have become so large, distant and unresponsive to people's lives and concerns that our communities are now, to a serious degree, ungoverned. Administrate neglect and private actions have endangered the safety and justice of our communities. We believe it is the responsibility of citizens in our democratic republic to govern the affairs of their own neighborhood communities in common deliberation, with binding jurisdictional power, and in constitutional relationship to other communities.

- *Herber M. Levine*

iv. *Context is all:* no culture exists alone. Every organization of scope and complexity is a compound of cultures. The relative power of each culture on comparison to the others determines what it can do. The solution to the hierarchy problem, therefore, is to surround it with a sufficient force of other cultures to mitigate its excesses without depriving it of the ability to maintain order.

- *Aaron Wildausky*

v. 'Public choice theorists prefer decentralized price or market systems, because they make fewer demands on the decision maker by reducing the scale of the system of choices to be coped with.

-Summary by Robert T.Golembiewski

vi. 'The major expression of development administration in the field is decentralization, the unclogging of business at the centre. Development administration, therefore, is not only the administration of development, it is the development of administration.

- George F. Gant

vii. 'Decentralisation is primary means of combining the best elements in bureaucracy and enterprise.

- Marshal E. Dimock

It will be seen that the inadequacy of 'overhead' democracy is viewed not only in the perspective of a more soulful version of democracy, but also in that of greater organizational efficiency; the latter is a function of the countervailing power of conflicting organsiational cultures, of in- built dynamism and reform orientations, and of an environment facilitative of greater innovation, enterprise and effectiveness.

4. To an extent, the above tilts in favour of basic political values, and certain positive aspects associated therewith, probably overstated. That all structures, including bureaucratic ones, are bound to have negative features must be regarded as axiomatic. All the same, it would be instructive to have a glance at the negative aspects of decentralization.

i) Weaker sections have suffered under Panchayati Raj because of its domination by dominant castes.

ii) Panchayati Raj has adversely affected administrative efficiency, and weakened the procedural safeguards for rule of law, on account of political pressures, interference, favouritism and victimization.

iii) 'Democratic decentralization is no substitute for faithful agents, for it cannot create what does not exist. And it is mocking at the poor to ask them to perform this role. The whole scheme of democratic decentralization is one gigantic and dishonest attempt to "decentralize" responsibility and to conveniently pass the buck' 25.

-Lalit Uniyal

Answers to these criticisms are inherent in the enunciations of Ripon, Gandhi and Nehru, quoted earlier. We will, therefore, attempt a brief explication. First, the point relating to dominant castes. Their domination of Panchayati Raj Institutions is a fact. One must, however, remember that dominant castes derived their power from an antecedent social order (caste and Jajmani systems, agrarian structure, etc.), in existence for centuries before the introduction of the Panchayati Raj system. Panchayati Raj has had the merit or demerit of bringing to the fore, and to the forum of public opinion, the realities of an antecedent power structure, perhaps in a starker form. These realities would be there without Panchayati Raj. Some 'noble' souls could possibly contend that had there been no Panchayati Raj, and the opportunities for aggrandizement and oppression it offered, the power of dominant castes would have withered away, through voluntary acts of self-obnegation. Similar souls in the bureaucratic set-up have argues that civil servants (being endowed with 'political neutrality', and with greater nobility, or a more progressive outlook) would 'objectively' carry out the constitutional mandate of transforming society in the direction of egalitarianism, social justice and economic freedom; in other words, in the interest of the weaker sections. It is unlikely that most thinkers and social scientists would go along with such 'noble' souls. The logic is fairly simple. If these souls are angelic in their self-congratulatory effervescence, their political realism would be suspect. Instances of changes in power structure through acts of self-obnegation are far too few to sustain a tenable generalization. When one talks of general trends, it is more likely that a larger number of these 'noble' souls have a shrewd appreciation of the threats posed by below the 'overhead' democratic processes to their respective power configurations, and quote the scriptures in order to stall, or weaken the impact of, these threats. In that case, their political motives would be suspect. The dictum—'the good in man makes democracy possible, and the bad in man makes democracy necessary' – accommodates sufficient scope for the free play of noble human impulses across the board. But claims about 'nobility'. 'Political neutrality' and objectivity, on the part of the power configurations mentioned above, do little justice to the aggregate picture of human nature, and the dynamics of socio-political change strongly conditioned thereby. The only antidote to abuse of power, endemic in all structures, including democratic ones, is increasing the capacity of the people, as Gandhiji said long age, to check and control it. As a vehicle of this capacity, Panchayati Raj had the potential, as Gandhiji foresaw, to weaken the feudal order of rajas and zamindars. Ripon had a similar perception vis-à-vis the 'autocratic' district administration.

Now, students of political sociology are in a position

to confirm their insights and anticipation.

i) Wider democratic processes and Panchayati Raj have had the effect of weakening the 'old' order of dominant castes, by intensifying factionalism among these castes, by shuffling elites periodically in rather dramatic ways, and by broadening the socio-economic base of elite recruitment in favour of those with a better educational background, greater perceived empathy on their part for poorer groups, and better accessibility. Even if the leaders are still largely dawn from the 'dominant castes', they have lost, or shed, some of the older feudal flavour,. Caste nomenclature, pure and simple, does not mean much unless the changing contours of socio-political evolution are given due weight.

ii) Much, however, depends upon the way the issue relating to the increase in the capacity of the people to influence the shape of things is answered. While it would be difficult to explain the impact of democratic processes from this point of view during the relatively latent phase stretchable up to mid-seventies, it is abundantly clear that since the elections of 1977 we have had dramatic confirmations of the voters' capacity time and again. Every political party has reasons to feel that it is kept on tenter hooks; it should consider itself fortunate if it is elected for more than one term.

The researches done by the present writer suggest that rural voters take, generally speaking panchayati Raj elections more seriously. In such a milieu, to interpret the changing realities of the present with reference to the facts of an earlier evolutionary dispensation would be obviously erroneous. Mahatma Gandhi has been amply vindicated: and so has been Ripon's optimism about the impact of political and public education, after a short period of failure. Now that phase of failure is behind us.

(iii) The above analysis warrants the broad conclusion that democracy in India gas arrived, despite the persistence of problem of transition, in some places and at some times in aggravated forms. Democracy, like other remedies, cannot cure all ills, in fact, potent remedies often have worrying side effects. In order that our worries about these side effects do not could our appreciation would be: from the standpoint of the common people (weaker sections) is there a better friend than democracy? (and at the local levels, which matter more, Panchayati Raj? Our answer is that votes, and the collective capacity to determine their disposition in desired directions, empower the common people to confront their rulers, and bend them to their collective will in broader or specific ways depending upon the context. Democracy responds better not because of the efficacy of the collective will. The advantage (or the magic, if one might say so) lies in the congruence of the message (democracy) with the medium (democracy). The message of democracy (preamble to the constitution) cannot be realized through a bureaucratic or pre-democratic medium. Goal displacements, or distortions, inevitable in all organizational forms, on account of limitations of perspectives and pursuit of self and group aggrandizement, have a much better change of getting reduced (but not eliminated altogether) through the self-corrective processes of democracy, than otherwise. In this scientific methodology. Both share the advantages of cumulative growth through open-ended exchanges of ideas and experience. Because of this, as also the proven inadequacies or perversities of dogmatism and authoritarianism, democracy can be considered a better bet-a bad form of government like all other forms of government, but still better than rest. Here lie the macro, largely latent, efficiencies of the system.

(iv) Inefficiencies arising from 'interference', and down the form and substance of 'rule of law' are real in large parts of the country, and cannot be wished away, even after discounting overstatements coloured by perceptions of threat to the power and privileges the bureaucracy is used to. This would be more disconcerting if we take into account; the fact that the modern 'administrative state' has to be, to quote millet, 'well served by its administrative apparatus'. Quite a segment of the Indian bureaucracy, however, overshoots the mark by suggesting that to have an effective Panchayati Raj is to damage this apparatus. On this issue, global experience can hardly be said to support their exaggerated fears. Even so, Millett's following advice could be considered apposite: "In the administrative state, control of the bureaucracy by political institutions is matter of some finesse and subtlety". Considering the pervasive public dissatisfaction with bureaucracy in India (with its massive corruption, and widespread discourtesy, delays and inefficiency), contributing to a blurring of the distinction between legitimate intervention and illegitimate interference, one is tempted to say, vice-versa. The organizational culture on either side has advantages which need to be pressed into service in the larger public interest. The dransformative role of the political side should conceivably have a far higher salience. Rainy Kithara puts things in perspective when he says: pantheist, local cooperatives and their like can be used for both democratic and elite dominated ends. By themselves they are not decentralizing. If they are to be made instruments of a decentralized order, they need to be steered in that direction by a larger model of transformative political along a variety of dimensions. This would presumably include the bureaucratic dimension, which, if adequately exposed to the value thrust of Tran formative politics would acquire that sensitivity, understanding and courage, necessary for relating exercise of administrative responsibilities to intimations of the constitutional order and nuances of socio-political development. That democratic processes intensify the mechanism of transformation, to monitor and correct the course of development. If this is appreciated, alit uniyals objection to using decentralization as a passing the back device can be well taken and effectively tackled. His wider point regarding faithful agents first is something to which the creator alone could respond satisfactorily. The poor, on their part, have used their part have used their votes fairly effectively to throw out those considered to be deficient, at intervals short enough to make the pace of political development faster. The elites might mock at them; but their votes have mocked at the elites. Not surprisingly, therefore, the rural voters, while being very vocal about the failures and shortcomings of Panchayati Raj, come out with a resounding 'no' when the question of scrapping Panchayati Raj is posed to them. They know in their heart of hearts that Panchayati Raj (with its leaders being far more accessible) is a better bet than bureaucracy. If making the best of a bad bargain, through the only power-conferring medium known to them (democracy) is a virtue, it deserves appreciation rather than derision. It would be worse to mislead them into narrower alleys where elites with pre-liberal orientations are lying in wait to exploit remnants of their gullibility to the advantage of their respective power configurations. Not many seem to appreciate the fact that the 'mere' right to vote is a significant advance towards social equality, in a society characterised by some of the most outrageous assaults on human dignity.

All this still does not conclusively answer the point regarding the dominance of dominant castes. Thanks to the pressures generated by democracy, some structural and other changes have brought about greater political equality, not uniformly but in a broad measure. The common people should, and in a sense, do know haw voting enables them to influence things from a collective 'vantage' point. Ironically, civil servants emphasise this point (regarding 'dominance') more vocally, as if their social background and interests were qualitatively different! When the chips are down, one knows where their cleverly camouflages premises lead them to (the instances of bureaucratic indifference or hamhandedness vis-à-vis scheduled castes/tribes are fact too many to bear meticulous documentation). Here again, democracy, by bringing the realities of dominance to the level of public awareness, has invited or necessitated political responses. Among them, reservation of positions in the Panchayati Raj system can go a long way in fostering an environment of participation and security for the weaker sections. This has already happened in some states. If extended to the entire country, a major 'counter point' would lose its edge, if not relevance, fairly soon. Some comic relief should be welcomed as a part of the human drama in case those advancing the 'counter point' oppose such reservations!

5. Despite these and other difficulties, Panchayati Raj has performed rather well over the decades. Generally speaking, it has performed better in states where it was allowed to function, through structural, policy and administrative support. Several high power committees have noted with appreciation the direct and indirect impetus given by Panchayati Raj to the implementation of programmes relating to roads, educational and health facilities, rural electrification and agricultural development in general, in terms of both pace and content. These gains from the standpoint of the poorer groups have to be balanced against the misuse of power by Panchayati Raj leaders to benefit their castemen, party men and political supporters, and acts of discrimination against those belonging to weaker sections numerous enough to fuel protest movements (e.g., of 'backward classes') against the landed gentry. The important point is that because of the availability of Panchayati Raj as a democratic structure, the discontent was converted into aggregate electoral results characterized by extensive shuffling. There are here intimations of the rejection of the culture of accommodation—a condition of economic development which bureaucracy, strongly oriented to accommodation, is structurally ill-fitted to bring about. In fact, the bureaucratic hostility towards Panchayati Raj is partly attributable to the 'liberalization' of administrative life, in the sense of the penetration of liberal values into the domain of 'citizen-administration' relations, and the resultant assertiveness on the part of citizens, some of whom might carry their assertiveness to crude manifestations. On the whole, as in the case of economic performance, the net effect of rejection of accommodation with preliberal power configurations would be

improvement in administrative performance. The important point is that Panchayati Raj should be viewed as a 'social direction system' (in terms of 'foundational' issues, as Amartya Sen would put it), and not merely as an administrative entity. The following broad conclusions of a study ('Factors Affecting Development of the Panchayati Raj system') directed by the present author, throw further light on the issue under discussion.

i) A perspective on Panchayati Raj with a pronounced bias towards 'administrative instrumentalism' is reflective of a weaker political will, leading to a weaker system, than one characterized by a stronger commitment to foundational issues. The strength of such commitment would be an important factor contributing to the development of Panchayati Raj.

ii) As an institutional focus for evoking, sustaining and raising the level of interest in, and understanding of, aspects of rural development, Panchayati Raj has come to occupy significant place in the minds of large majority of respondents.

iii) A high degree of psychic identity with Panchayati Raj, coupled with a critical attitude towards gaps in leadership and performance and a supportive attitude towards its continuance and strengthening, are factors which would facilitate the development of the 'Panchayati Raj system on sounder lines. Panchayati Raj has contributed to raising the capabilities of the people vis-à-vis antecedent political arrangements and the use of democratic structures to register more exacting demands. Conservative proclivities of elites, such

As they are (at any given time), will weaken further as the trend gains greater momentum.

(iv) A structurally sounder system of panchayati raj makes a substantial contribution to making the development administration machinery more responsive and accessible, and to promoting a more cooperative relationship between and non-official.

We have desisted from citing statistical data about rural development in this or that sector, and in this or that state. From monsoons through all the factors listed by Galbraith, we have a complex matrix of factors. It would be an impossible task to locate the positive or negative contribution of pachayati Raj to various dimensions of development. Perhaps the best way of looking at the overall picture is to see if the contribution of Panchayati Raj to the weakening of the culture of accommodation, to the improvements in the levels of public satisfaction (to, in the Jargon of management, effectiveness), and to up gradation of administrative performance, have been substantial. As further discussion would show, available knowledge, insights and evidence warrant a positive response.

6. Procedure-cum-ego-cum-interest cent red views of administrative efficiency can be said to be narrow to do justice to its multi-dimensionality discussed above. This is particularly true of the district administration where the problems of the cutting-edge find their most disconcerting expression. The antecedent feudal- colonial ethos, still relatively strong in states without a sturdy tradition of Panchayati Raj, has to be squarely faced for what it does, in the manner done by a liberal viceroy, Lord Ripon more than a century ago. Failure to do so, and take remedial measures, has meant the persistence

of widespread dissatisfaction, even hatred, vis-à-vis the autocratic district administration. Some patches of technical or procedural efficiency have been massively overshadowed by gaps in empathy and corruption. This again is not a politically neutral proposition. One women serpanch from Maharashtra, a person belonging to weaker sections told the late Prime Minister, Rajiv Gandhi, that earlier for getting things like roads, schools and electricity, the rural people had to beg before officers (e.g.BDO). She asked: why should we beg? And added: if we have Panchayats we do not have to beg; Bureaucrats of the older autocratic variety might try to skirt the political issue raised here by clear appeals to some selective aspects of efficiency. In the view taken by the sarpanch, the responsiveness embodied in a democratic structure has implications both for effectiveness (public satisfaction) and efficiency in the sense of overall developmental performance. The spectrum of scholarly opinion, culled from recent writings, illustrate some dimensions of the proposition.

(i) Administrative responsiveness depends not only on the public servants capacity to respond to public needs through formal mechanisms, it also depends on their inclination to respond, whether through formal or informal means.

- *Kenneth Kernaghan*

(ii) In its decisions, procedures and actions, the rural poor do not seem to matter much to the bureaucracy, it is still quite common to consider them last of all. The poor continue to be viewed as passive recipients of benefits from development projects and not as part pants in the real sense of the term.

- *Hari Mohan Mathur*

(iii) A top-down/bottom-up flow of communication and initiative is recognized as the main ingredient in responsive and account-able administrative capacity. The tendency for policy making to be highly centralized in national administrative structures is further recognized as a major constraint on attempts to nature responsive and accountable distractive capacity.

- *David Fashole Luke*

(iv) Access, citizen participation, and political responsiveness are all expected to increase with political decentralisation.

- *David O.Porter and Eugene A.Olsen*

In relation to the ground realities in India, where the venality of the petty bureaucracy and arrogance of the superior bureaucracy lend a contextual poignancy to the urge for responsive administration, the points made above can be said to have greater relevance. This dormant urge found a powerful expression in Rajiv Gandhi dynamic initiatives with regard to responsive administration, for about three years from 1986. In his address to the Fifth workshop of distinct magistrates on responsive administration, at Coimbatore, on the June 18, 1988, he dew pointed attention to the systemic nature of the underlying problem, beyond simplification of procedures was insufficiently responsive, the basic reason is that it is not sufficiently representative asserting that the major reality of post-independence India is the assertion of the people will he reminded those who wanted the power and authority of the district collector to be restored by some sort of decree or fiat central or state government, that the attempt to preserve the office of district magistrate as kind of island of benevolent paternalism rising above the surging waves of democracy is what has resulted in the District Magistrates island being eróded. A good many (for too may?) officers in this category have tended to look the other way (away the surging waves of democracy) with an astoundingly illiberal indifference to policy pronouncements on the systemic thrust of democratic decentralization, and the tasks of economic growth bound up with it. A good deal has been said on this aspect. The eighth plan approach paper of the Janet Daly led regime summed it up in the following words. Democratic decentralization which is at the heart of the institutional changes envisaged, will need to cover both political and economic process, (pp. 10-11). Stressing the crucial importance of revitalizing Panchayati Raj institutions with direct command over a sizeable volume of finance and the freedom and flexibility to decide how best it can be used for local development, encompassing planning and implementation of economic and social development programmes (pp. 14-15).

7. Apart from responsiveness, and all that it means for the effectiveness and efficiency of development administration, the trend towards sustainable development reinforces the case for decentralization in ways unthinkable till the politics of greening came on the horizon in recent decades. The debate is simplex in its thematic range and nuances. From our point of view here, the basic issue is the politics of development: the question of choosing between an ecologically perilous model of industrial development, fuelled by consumerism, and an ecologically sensible model in which sustainability and social justice become the watch words. Apart from violence and wars, the consequences of the former include high levels of poverty and

unemployment in development countries. If we, in India correct these consequences through the latter (is there any real choice in the matter?) we will not only be tackling the ecological crisis but making a major contribution towards the solution of the problems of unemployment and poverty. And unemployment in developing counties. If we, in India, correct these consequences through the latter (is there nay real choice in the matter?) we will not only be tacking the ecological crisis but making a major contribution towards the solution of the problems of unemployment and poverty. Secure in the belief about their political neutrality, some bureaucrats instructively support the conventional model of industrial development, with its high-tech and high centralization attributes: here lies the power to influence the course of things in accordance with their interests and political perspectives, no matter what happens to our fragile bio-sphere (years ago, in his future shock, Toffler Wanted us against technocratic bureaucratic myopia). The political of ecology and green economics have compelled attention to the integral connection between sustainable development and decentralization. The world commission on environment and Development provides an authoritative exposition of this connections; sustainability requires the enforcement of wider responsibilities for the impacts of decisions. This requires changes in the legal and institutional frameworks that will enforce the common interest.... The law alone cannot enforce common interest. It principally needs community knowledge and support, which entails greater public participation in decisions that affect the environment. This is best secured by decentralized management of resources upon which local communities depend, and giving these communities an effective say over the use of these resources. It will also require promoting citizens initiatives, empowering peoples organizations, and strengthening local democracy. Here is another vital dimension of the case for Panchayati Raj a more local scale of economic and political activity, blending green economics with the politics of peace, liberation and ecology. The cost of prevarication or delay would be exceedingly heavy in terms of damaging the life-sustaining capacity of the Earth. It would also mean a gross neglect of intergenerational equity. We do not inherit the earth from our ancestors: we borrow it from our children, these are the imperatives behind the dictum-think globally and act locally. And one might paraphrase, behind Panchayati Raj.

8. If Panchayati Raj means a frame of reference as wide as global, some strong decentralist trends in the west particularly in the wake of the neighborhood councils movement do deserve serious attention. The movement brought into sharper focus the gap between the rhetoric but also of local government the proponents protested against the way both bureaucrats and councilors (in the local government system) considered themselves as us and the ordinary citizens or rate payers as they. The movement resulted in the establishment of Neighbourhood centers. The movement resulted in the establishment of neighborhood centers (e.g. in the UK) equipped to provide prompt and courteous service to citizens as near their doorsteps as possible. The following formulation bring out the flavour of the new trends quite eloquently.

(i) Decentralization is a policy of confrontation. It confronts the despair and local government. It provides better, more accessible services and offers people an opportunity to have control over their own lives. Decentralization is not merely a bureaucratic change in the way that councils provide their services. It is a change in the philosophy of local government. It is giving power to local people.

(ii) Going local initiatives challenge the dispersal of power on may fronts. The targets can range from challenging the balance of power between constituents and the town hall, to challenging the internal dispersal of power existing within the organization of local authorities. This distinguishes going local from other decentralizing initiatives like area-based management.

Flavors, however, is different from menu. A good analysis of the decentralist trends in the west can be found in L.J. Sharpe (ed) decentralist trends in western democracies (London: Sage, 1979). Introductory papers (training material) of the institute of local government studies, university of Birmingham, contain a good deal of useful information. One of the papers draws attention to the point that while the administrative system tends to look inward to its task, the elected members provide an alternative information source (complaints are a critical element in the councilors role) the fact of election opens up debate within the authority to the public outside. This is an interesting variation on the theme of complementarily of organizational cultures expounded by Wildausky, touched upon earlier. It may perhaps be decades before the climate of opinion in India and the organizational culture of the bureaucracy, could be said to be ready for assimilating such a soulful view of citizen-administration relations. But given the global sweep of democratic upsurge, and the compulsion of green economics behind decentralization, speculation about a speedier progress in this direction may not be unrealistic.

9. Viewed against the background of the overall perspective, and a number of specific points articulated above, the task of identifying areas of improvement vis-à-vis the Panchayati Raj system should become easier.

(i) Certain degree of clarity and commitment at the highest political levels have already been achieved, this is reflected in the moves to provide constitutional support for strengthening Panchayati Raj financially and otherwise. Eventually, resistance from those not favorably inclined towards Panchayati Raj (in the representative rubric, they include a section of the members of state legislative assemblies), because of perceptions of threat to power and prestige, can be expected to weaken sooner than later. How ever, countering the illiberal assumptions of some segments of bureaucratic structures, will pose a more serious problem, solution to which would entail political direction of a more decisive kind, Tran formative rather than procedural in nature.

(ii) As far rural people are concerned, a reassuringly high level of psychic identification with Panchayati Raj, and critical support to it in an evolving environment increasingly demanding in its tone and temper, should regarded as valuable assets, and a vital part of the success of the system. A similar sense of identification on the part of the representative and bureaucratic segments of our public life is called for. It must be clearly realized that decentralization is half of the game of efficiency and effectiveness (public satisfaction), the other half spanning contextual variables and details to which mature attention would be useful.

(iii) The grievance about the domination of dominant casts can be tackled to a large extent through the system of reservations for SC/s ST/s and OBCs, through the impact of direct elections, through the operation of democratic mechanisms in the direction of non-inscriptive values, through spin-offs of representative bureaucracy: and through Tran formative politics. There is an element of inexorability about these factors.

(iv) Evolving a culture of togetherness between the non-official and official wings of Panchayati Raj, and promoting better structural and behavioral adjustments among them, is bound up with the tasks discussed above. The prime minister recently described the bureaucracy as a trained animal which would do its allotted task well, if the political direction is clear. It was an insightful observation. As an interest group, the bureaucracy would understandably use the resources available to it to block the course of decentralized democracy to the extent it is perceived to threaten its interests viewed in a narrow interest group frame of deference. The experience of Panchayati Raj in the country clearly shows that where the political direction (reflected in legislation) is learn, it not only cooperates, but develops an enthusiastic orientation towards Panchayati Raj. Numerous civil servants, with experience of working with Zillah Perishad in states like

Gujarat, Maharashtra, West Bengal and Karnataka, have shared this enthusiasm during periods of unambiguous political support. As goal displacement is a universal phenomenon, and as democratic processes have been more effective than other factors in pushing both non-officials and officials closer to goals, it might be said (modifying a statement of Marx in another context) that by acting on Panchayati Raj and reacting to it, both sets of functionaries would change themselves. Democratic ethos does quite a bit, in an incremental way, to their management software (leadership and communication styles, vide in search of excellence), a vital component of efficiency.

(v) Macro solution of course, are no substitute for micro ones, in the sense that what is necessary is not sufficient. Guarding against rash generalization, one might refer to the tendency among certain types of non-officials to indulge in acts of arbitrary decision-making. A similar tendency, among comparable personality types, is not totally absent among officials. Though on this too, the evolution of democratic ethos (already visible to warrant optimism) is bound to have a salutary effect. Adoption of sophisticated mechanisms of planning would reduce the extent of arbitrariness in the Panchayato Raj System, to the relief of power holders themselves eventually. Shrewd persons on the either side know this to be a fact.

(vi) A similar ingenuity vis-à-vis the problem of corruption (considered to be, wrongly in our opinion, more rampant in the Panchayati Raj system), is possible; but one must remember that the intensity of corruption here is a reflection of that at higher political levels: political parties and individual candidates are driven by a sense of insecurity to spend huge amounts to 'bribe voters', just in case: some modes of political campaigning also involve heavy expenditure. With 'recovery of costs' after victory contributing in a major way to the problem of corruption, it would be a distinct public gain if all concerned make the election system far less expensive; it should be easier in that many voters vote the way they like irrespective of the amounts spent, given the periodicity of elections in a multi-level democracy, social costs on this account can be reduced if governments at different levels cooperate to provide the needed infrastructure (like places and facilities for facilities for public meetings) on a permanent basis.

(vii) All the factors discussed above cumulatively lead to raising the level of public opinion to a point where corruption and violations of the processes of rule of law would become increasingly difficult. The weapon of elections is weakening of legitimacy, and no structure caring for public esteem can afford to take big risks here. In this environmental setting, procedural safeguards can be expected to be far more effective. As far as reduction of corruption through better financial management is concerned, every Zilla Parishad should have an officer of the Rank of Deputy Accountant General, belonging to the IAAS, with the enactment of the new Seventy Second Constitution Amendment Bill, the budget of an average Zilla Parishad is likely to be of the order of fifty crores, equivalent of the budget of several universities put together. Hence, having a senior officer of the IAAS should not be considered a needless expenditure. Further, a number of district level officers have experimented with systems of 'office management'. The best combination can be adopted with a view to improving both responsiveness and behavioural rectitude. Such a system would send clear signals to persons both within and outside the organization as to where the substance of accountability lies: to the people.

(viii) With such an accountability, and their procedural appurtenances, striking roots in popular consciousness, numerous incremental improvements and adjustments would make internal administrative reform a continuous proposition, leading to improvements in the management of hardware (Structural aspects) as well. A triangular interaction among the people in general, and officials and non-officials, would help inject into the organizational culture some 'social action' inputs, considered a little inconvenient by officials as well as non-officials. Both, it should not be forgotten, are power holders, prone to goal displacements unless brought nearer the track. More than several other kinds of inputs, it is inputs of the kind mentioned above which should provide the basic rationale for Panchayati Raj from an administrative point of view. Establishment of grievance cells would lend greater dynamism to the triangular interaction.

LOCAL PLANNING FOR EDUCATIONAL DEVELOPMENT

Introduction

The concept of local level planning is a relatively recent addition to the toolbox of planners and development specialists. It may be considered as a logical extension of the national and regional planning processes in vogue for the last several decades. An alterative explanation for its emergence may be traced to the needs and aspirations of the local communities. By bringing planning to the grassroots level, the inadequacies of national and regional planning process are sought to be blunted, if not completely removed.

Local planning may also be looked upon as a strategy for below. As such it is utilized to mobilize local resources; to ensure popular participation; and to forge a strong link between governmental and non-governmental orgnisations engaged in development initiatives, planning, and management.

Despite the growing popularity of local level planning, in methodological terms it is still in infancy. It is so close to the people; so directly concerned with the needs, aspirations and problems of the people; and so much dependent on what the people think and do, that it is highly subject to human factors. While in national planning, the focus of attention might be on macro-framework building and the growth of the GDP, planning at the local level is faced with such mundance problems as provision of food and potable water; construction of school building, link roads, water channels. These problems are seen in real human terms not in terms of percentages and ratios.

As compared to national and regional planning, local planning is characteristically weak in Institutional support and organisation I most developing countries. This is because of the highly centralized and inverted pyramid structure of the government agencies and signal lack of institutions which can take community responsibilities for panning and development.

Aside from the Organisational and Institutional aspects of local planning another important factor to consider is the linkage of the local plan t both the horizontal and vertical axes of the governmental politico-administrative hierarchy. This linkage, among others, defines the explicit connection of a local plan to other plans—local, regional and national, particularly on points of priorities, policies and strategies. Note that the vertical and horizontal linkage should have two temporal dimensions: at a point of time and through time.

The main hurdles in the way of local planning can be summarized in the following terms:

a. "If national policies to decentralize the process of development were not undertaken with political will, that could severely limit the achievements of local-level planning, for the instance, in the form of budgetary difficulties, landownership laws that facilitate exploitation, unfavorable terms of trade leading to low purchasing power, of rural communities and lack of coverage of risk owing to uncertainties in agriculture resulting in less than optimum production.

b. The civil administration largely operated within law and order and control parameters rather than the promotion of rural development or the sharing of authority and responsibilities with the rural poor. Thus, even with the best of intentions, bureaucraciesvwith traditional orientation could hamper the processes of local-level planning.

c. The lack of willingness and methodology to organize and institutionalize the participation of the people, particularly where rural communities were heterogeneous in nature and structure.

d. The limited managerial skills of local people and lack of organizations for planning and development.

e. The inadequate planning and management competencies of administrators operating at the local level.

f. The difficulty of matching local needs with nationally determined priorities and of relating that to available resources and budgets; and

g. The long-established dependent attitudes of the rural population.

Local planning aims at the total development of the area or communities living in an area marked by commonality, inter dependence solidarity. It is people centered and trains them to take responsibilities of development on their own shoulders. In many respects, local planning is a corrective strategy to remove distortions generated by technocratic and bureaucratic central planning processes at the national and regional levels.

Local Level Planning in India

Panchayati Raj Institutions (PRIs)

The history of Local Planning in India can be traced back to the Decentralization Commission (1907) which recommended the creation of Village Panchayats as the lowest level administrative units of the government. It used the term local self-government and was designed to supercede the informal autonomy of Indian village government. It became the lowest tier in the pyramidical structure the British created to rule the country.

After independence the situation did change but only marginally. The Indian Constitution in Article 40 deals with local self-government as if following the recommendations of 1907 commission. Later, taking inspiration from Balwantray Mehta Committee report, PRIs became instruments of democratic decentralization in the country. Then followed the Asoka Mehta Committee report and several others. But the system did not change in substance. During 1959–65 the PRIs were in ascendancy; then set in the phase of stagnation (1965-69): 1969-84 can be said to be the phase of decline. One may now add the fourth phase i.e. the phase of revitalization which began around 1984.

The Asoka Mehta Committee Observed

"Panchayati Raj Institutions are dominated by economically and socially privileged sections of society and have as such facilitated the emergence of oligarchical forces yielding no benefits to weaker sections. The performance of the PRIs has also been vitiated by political factionalism rendering development thrusts either warped or diluted corruption; inefficiency; scant regard for procedures; political interference in day-today administration; parochial loyalties; motivated actions; power construction instead of service consciousness-all these seriously limited the utility of Panchayati Raj for the average villager.

It recommended extensive decentralization of power to district and the next lower tiers i.e. Mandal (cluster of Villages) and the village. But not much was done to follow it up. The G.V.K. Rao Committee was appointed in 1980 to suggest ways of revamping rural local government. The committee reported in 1985 recommending pivotal role for the district level bodies. L.M. Singhvi Committee appointed by the Ministry of Rural Development reported in 1986 and resurrected the nearly forgotten Gram Sabha Comprising all the inhabitants of the village, and called it as the embodiment of direct democracy. It recommended vesting the Panchayati Raj bodies with constitutional status by inserting a separate chapter in the Constitution of India so as to make identity and integrity of the Panchayati Raj institutions reasonably and substantially inviolate. Instead of Mandal Samitis, it suggested the establishment of Nyaya Panchayats for a cluster of villages.

Following the above recommendations, various state governments in accordance with their own political and other conveniences established three-tier Panchayati Raj institutions. They could be grouped under two models.

Model I	-	*Model II*
Zilla Parishad	-	Zilla Parishad
Block Samiti	-	Taluka Development Board
Nyaya Panchayat	-	Mandal Samiti
Gram Panchayat/Gram Sabha	-	Gram Panchayat/Gram Sabha

In model I, Nyaya Panchayats and Gram Sabhas have only notional importance. Similarly, in model II Taluka Development Boards and Gram Sabhas have only notional importance, although in practice, the Taluka Development Boards in Karnataka, due to historical and administrative reasons have tended to take over much of the roles of the Mandal Samitis.

Model II is prevalent in states like Karnatak and Anadhra Pradesh. Karnataka, for example, has transferred almost all planning and development functions and personnel at and below the district level to the elected Panchayti Raj bodies and devolved adequate resources for development. The regulatory functions like law and order are left with the collector of the district. There are sectoral standing committees. Heads of various functional departments like agriculture, health education are the secretaries of the relevant standing committee of the Zilla Parishad (nine in number) Presided over by the elected members of the Zilla Parishad.

It would be worth noting that the Karnataka Panchayati Raj bodies are fully elected ones. All members of the Zilla Parishad and Mandal Samitis are directly elected. Members of Parliament and State Legislatures are only coopted members. There is reservation of seats for SC and ST (in proportion to their population), women (25%), and backward classes (2 seats). The dhyaksha and Upadhyaksha of Zilla Parishad have the status of Minister of state and deputy Minister, respectively. A new functionary called chief secretary to the Zilla Parishad drawn form IAS cadre looks after the planning and development functions of the district.

Model I is prevalent in States like U.P. with Zilla Parishd at the apex and Block Samitis and Gram

Panchayats down below. Thee is provision of Nyaya Panchyats and Gram Sabhas but they exist only on paper. Under this model the Deputy Commissioner or District Magistrate as he is usually called, is the Secretary of the Zilla Parishad. Chairman/Adhyaksha of the Zilla Parishad is responsible for district development planning. The Adhyksha of the Zilla Parishad and chairman of the Block Samiti are elected indirectly. Money and muscle power play major roles in the election of these functionaries.

Other states have followed one of the two models with variations to suit local and political conveniences. For example, in west Bengal, the Gram Panchayats have acquired far more powers and authority for development; in Maharashtra and Gujarat, Zilla Parishads have done an excellent job. There are cases of success and failures in both models.

Planning Process

While considerable progress can be said to have been made in establishing popular institutions for local planning, systematic planning process is yet to make Panchayati Raj institutions statutory and third tier of the federal structure of the country, need for systematization of the planning process to get optimum results from the changes in offing is urgently called for. As far as planning is concerned, none of the two models has scored a good grade. The choice is between the bad and the worse or worst. The tendency to change tiers and names of the institutions with the change in the political complexion of the government, is not only unhealthy but also a dangerous practice. The real change involves not only administrative decentralization but also devolution of power, authority and resources.

Putting IAS officers as chief secretaries of Zilla Parishads and conferring on the chairman the label of Ministers of State gives only a decent label t container full of garbage and brings to the grassroot level the elitist culture which characterizes the upper tiers of the government. The grass root level organizations—the Gram Sabha and Grama Panchayats—have been weakened and marginalized and in states like UP and Bihar, have been handed over to the local goons, musclemen and thug recruited as active members of political parties—both ruling and non-ruling.

It has to be realized that it is in the villages that grassroot democracy has to thrive to promote local level planning with each household as the basic unit of concern. And if the development progrmmes have been most effective in West Bengal, it were because the beneficiaries were selected by the village Panchayats which are manned by people less known for muscle power but more for service eventhough biased towards the ruling party ideology. There is informal 'social audit' in an ideology based local orgnisation. In other states where politics is marked by ideological aridity or fluidity, social audit is not possible and the musclemen rue the country-side.

Coming back to the local level planning process, one notices four model approaches. These are:

a. Technocratic Planning approach

b. Bureaucratic planning approach

c. Action Planning Approach

d. Gandhian approach

Technocratic approach. The technocratic planning is the brain child of academicians and management specialists. It aims at rationality in allocation of resources deals with processes and stages of planning; evolves policies and strategies for development; pays considerable attention to resources; analysis, project identification, formulation and evaluation; and spends lot of time and resources on evolving a well-structured development plan.

People's Participation in this type of exercise is limited to circulation of the draft plan for public opinion, and to holding meetings to inform the programmes under contemplation. In the 1970s, millions of dollars were spent in many developing countries under the auspices of the U and World Bank for this purpose. In man countries like Iran and Philippines, thousands of such documents prepared by consultants from Europe and the USA lie buried in the library stacks.

It is educative for planning students to brouse through these documents. They have used very sophisticated techniques-input-output analysis, game theory, linear programming etc. to arrive at development scenarios and potentialities. For those regions, which did not have the necessary data base, data were created under the plea that a good planner could not stop his work simply because of the inadequacy of data.

In India too we have a series of such district and block plans prepared by the academics. Unfortunately, most of these plans have not been implemented for the constraints outside the realm of reason were not taken into account by these well meaning experts.

Two disciplines—economics and geography—have played major roles in the technocratic planning exercises. The economists have developed plans with inter-sectoral consistency while the geographers with inter-space consistency. Methodologically, the economists have followed the national planning techniques while the geographers the regional planning techniques. For want of space , we cannot go into the details of these. Suffice it to say that the methodologies used have now become widely diffused and their strengths and weakness well known to the students of planning.

Bureaucratic approach. The second approach is the bureaucratic one. It continues to be in vogue allover the country. In the recent past, it has tried to incorporate a few terms and techniques from technocratic planners and some vocabulary from action planners to systematize it as practical approach to local level planning.

The bureaucratic approach relies heavily on line agencies for project identification. The projects so identified are pooled together and depending upon the availability of funds for different sectors from centrally sponsored schemes and state government allocations, they are pruned to constitute a list of projects. There is a write–up on each sector giving the benefits accruing from the selected projects. When put together, they constitute a district or block plan.

Unlike the technocratic plans, the bureaucratic plans eventhough badly formulated, are at least consulted in the process of development. Thus they fare better, for a plan which is not implemented is not a good plan at all. The pseudo plans prepared by the academics or the bureaucrats are there to see and not to act on and the money spent on them is a drain on the local resources which is always scarce. The existing administrative infrastructure is competent enough to prepare such documents. There is no need to have the office of district planner, or a district planning cell.

Action planning approach. The third type of planning exercise ie. action planning is resorted to by the voluntary agencies engaged in grassroot level planning and development. Action planning starts with a survey using participant observer method. Problems re understood and identified and their inter-relationships established. Report with the people, particularly the poor is built up. An action plan is prepared. It is discussed with the people and finally made into a people's plan with the voluntary agency going in the background to function as a catalytic agent. This plan is used to get funds for the projects taken up.

The methodology used centers on two approaches of first, it is the people who are put in the forefront. The aim is overall development and enabling people to stand on their own feet. And, two, only one or two projects are taken up as entry points. It is around these projects that other projects are built up.

Action planning is based on the premises that local problems are interrelated and no matter what the entry point, one has ultimately to tackle all problems. This approach gives lot of flexibility and offers scope for all disciplines to enter the field. So one can take up education; another health; the third housing and so on. The education planner for example, soon realizes that there are economic, social and other reasons for children not going to school, for high dropout rate; and for teachers not attending to their duties. He then develops projects to tackle those problems. While solving these second level problems he comes across third level problems and so on.

Thus instead of identifying projects technocratically or bureaucratically, the new projects roll out as action begins. These new projects are identified with and by the people. People become the planners, developers and the beneficiaries at the same time.

Gandhian approach. Since the mid-eighties, Panchayati Raj institutions (PRIs) are in the news again. Efforts, eventhough largely populistic, have been made to put these institutions on the rails again. The avowed objective is to usher in an area of democratic decentralization by creating a third tier in the system of government through constitutional amendments.

The name of Mahatma Gandhi as the votary of decentralization and village Panchayats has been frequently mentioned in this regard eventhough the model putforth is not in tune with the Gandhian concept of Gram Swaraj. It does not depart from the essentials of the pyramidical organizational structure which weakened the PRIs in the past and which, as stated earlier, is steeped in our colonial legacy.

Gandhiji advocated a participatory democracy at the village level. He was totally against a hierarchic structure with the top few sitting on the shoulders of the bottom many. He pleaded for the adoption of a model wherein the horizontal linkages and relationships were stronger than the vertical ones. He considered the humanity as the ocean and each individual, family, and community forming circles with unimpeded horizontal linkages and relationships. There could be no permanent boundaries in a fluid social order of equals. Each circle is important and determines the state of the ocean. Thus, in the Gandhi an set-up, it were the horizontal linkages and interrelations among the individuals, families and communities which constituted the bedrock of democratic decentralization: the vertical linkages are not so important, they are occasional, selective and specialized in nature.

The main attributes of the Gandhian approach can be summed up in the following terms:

1. Our goals should be to build a society based on Satya and Ahimsa. There is no need to dwell on these two terms. Suffice it to say that in such a society there is o scope and place for exploitation of one human being by another or nature by human beings.
2. The basic unit human society is a community which consists of a group of people living in close proximity sharing a variety of things in common and managing their day-to-day affairs without any interference from outside. These communities could be called villages in India.
3. In a world of such communities lrge cities would lose their present importance. That does not mean that there would be no cities. They would be there to cater to certain social-economic needs but their size would not acquire megapolitan scale. They will have certain industries and specialized services. But the amenities available there would not be better than those available in the rural communities and hence, people will not cluster in cities to make them grow disproportionately.
4. My ideal village will contain intelligent human beings. They will not live in dirt and darkness as animals. Men and women will be free and able to hold their own against anyone in the world. There will be neither plague, nor cholera, nor small-pox; no one will be idle; no one will wallow in luxury. Everyone will have to contribute his quota of manual labour. It is

possible to envisage railways, posts, telegraphs and the like. Today the villages are dung heaps. Tomorrow they will be like tiny gardens of Eden where dwell highly intelligent folks whom no one can deceive or exploit. When our villages are fully developed, there will be no dearth in them of men with a high degree of skill and artistic talent. There will be village poets, village artists, village architects, linguists and research workers. In short there will be nothing worth having, which will not be in the villages.

5. And hence "to serve our villages is to establish swaraj". Everything else is but an idle dream. Later in 1936, Gandhi said, "if the village perishes India will perish too. It will be no more India. Her own mission in the world will get lost. Thus, we see that the village for Gandhi was not the village that we see today." A Gandhian village was an indispensable and catalytic element of the grand design of new social order.

"If we try to work out necessary conditions for such a life (where no one rides over another's back) we are forced to the conclusions that the unit of society should be village or call it a manageable group of people who would in the ideal be self-sufficient in the matter of their vital requirements as a unit bound together in bonds of perpetual cooperation and inter-dependence".

As such while Gandhi saw a village as the hope of the future, his followers by and large saw it as a dung heap of superstitions and backwardness needing good dose of science, technology and urbanization. For Gandhi, Indian independence was a means to provide a new weapon in the hands of the oppressed the world over to free themselves, and village was the means to free human beings from economic and technological onslaughts of modern civilization.

As we look back now, we see that Gandhi was right. To a great extent. What have we made of this world? Our science and technology have acquired Bhasmasuri character for they were never tempered by spirituality. And our spirituality has become superstitious because it is no longer tempered by science. The science based spirituality of our Vedas and Upanishads is no longer valued. We are members of an ever growing society of desperate individuals each pursuing his own goals unmindful of its implications for the fellow beings. Gandhi could foresee that industrialism would ultimately breed alienated individuals and that is why he laid so much emphasis on village community and Gram Swaraj.

Local Planning for Educational Development

Education is key to development, it is all pervading. An ill-educated or uneducated society can never unfod its potentials. It is unfortunate that education is often seen s the learning of three Rs. But we live in this blessed great country of ours where even earning of the three Rs has becomes a privillage. We have the largest number of illiterates in the world. And this number is increasing everyday because our population growth is perhaps faster than the growth of literacy in the country.

Several commissions and committees have been appointed to examine the educational system of the country and to recommended policy measures to improve the situation. We cannot review the recommendations of all these committees here nor there is any need to do so. Suffice it to remark that nothing tangible has come out of these reports. Much of the energy was wasted in mergers, separations and remerges of different grades to conform to the changing patterns. Finally we settled down to 10+2+3 pattern without much change in the content, approach and style.

In matters of higher education the approach has remained selective laying emphasis on science and technology and newly relevant and emerging fields like management. The rest of the higher education sector has been allowed to expand without much of a qualitative change perhaps deliberately so that the vast number of boys and girls passing out of the secondary schools having no training for work could stay on for some time more.

Higher education in the country has never been linked to the manpower needs. It is the market which is the barometer and since market response is not quick in this sphere we either suffer from gluts or scarcities. Today we have more civil engineers than we need; and we have more trained teachers than we will ever need during the next several years. The market imbalance in other fields which are counted as soft have never been within manageable limits.

Coming down to the local level, we encounter a more depressing situation. At this level, we are concerned with primary education which incidentally also determines the level of literacy in the country. It is said that 4 to 6 years of good many continue their studies. The dropout rate for classes 1 to 8, is round 75 percent and for 1 to 5, about 65 percent. In other words, of the 100 children who join class 1 only 35 complete class 5 and only 25 class 8. Since a fairly large percentage drops out after a year or two, they no longer remain literate.

It is bad indeed that so many children dropout of the system. But if we take into court the facilities viable in the country, we would realize that but for the dropout, the system would have been choked to death.

The high dropout rate is due to external as well as internal factors. Among he external factors poverty and apathy of the parents is the major one. The internal factors pertain to the poor infrastructure, low quality and concern of teachers lack of extra–curricular activities, etc. Fifty per cent of the school buildings either do not exist or they exist only in name. There are no reading materials, many schools do not have even drinking water facilities.

While planning for primary education, we have over-emphasized subjects to be taught and the syllabus often aping the American and British Schools. We rejected the Indian model of basic education advocated by the greatest teacher of this century Mahatma Gandhi and went for the Western model. It my not be possible to reverse the gear but within the outlines of the system we have adopted, we have adopted, we can innovate and change the old order.

When we have so many millions of illiterates, so few children attending school, so poor facilities to handle the children once they enroll, would it then not be wiser to mound our system so that at least 3 Rs. are taught well. Should we not then shed much of the subjects which need lot of facilities and teach at least writing, reading and numeracy well. This used to be the case in olden times.

The fourth All India Educational Survey conducted

by NCERT for the year 1978–79 showed up that over 50 percent of the primary schools were without pucca buildings, 40 percent without block boards, 70 percent without library books and 85 percent without toilets. The next round of survey conducted in 1988-89 may show up some improvement but not substantial enough to change the situation for we know that allocation for primary education in the total outlay on education was reduced from 55.6 percent in the First Five Year plan to less than 30 percent in the Seventh Plan. Further, even these meager fund allocated for primary education were not spent on development, In 1978–79, 95.3 percent went for teachers' salaries, 1.9 percent for administration and supervision 1.7 percent for building and only 1.1 percent for other expenses. About 30 percent f the primary schools are single teacher schools. In such a dismal state of affairs, we expect the bys and girls to earn the ways to enter the 21st century.

Educational planning has been obscurantist in the country. Educationalists have concentrated on syllabus number of years of school, text books, pedagogy, etc. spatial planners have concentrated on the location of educational facilities using the growth center strategy. While efforts in these directions should continue and perhaps made more intensive, both the approaches lose meaning in the absence of new societal movement wherein everyone must become literate and every primary school must be well equipped within a given span of time. Unless there is a mass mobilization and large scale involvement of voluntary agencies, senior citizens and unemployed youth, India shall remain backward nation, it shall not be able to eradicate the curse of illiteracy from its body politic.

The Shanti Sen movement launched by the

Gandhigrm Rural institute is something in the right direction. Successful literacy progrmmes in Kottayam town and Ernakulam district point to the utility and efficacy of such a movement. These movements have to be launched at the local level—district, block, town, ward, village, when so many such movements begin, they would all converge into national movement.

Educational planning at the local level has to move out of the confines of curriculum and locational planning and plan for the use of local resources—human and others—to educate all.

Planning for the Village School

Given the above framework and perspectives for educational planning we can now discuss the concept and role of a village school and what can be done to invigorate these schools.

Kothari Commission (1964–66) gave the idea of school complex. The recommendation was accepted by the government and pilot projects were launched in a number of states. The commission recorded that there were 26000 secondary schools in India out of which 14000 were in rural areas at the beginning f the Fourth Five Year Pan. Similarly, there were 65000 middle schools and 360000 primary schools. The commission found these school in a integrated into school complexes. There was one secondary school in a radius of 8 to 16 km and within the catchments area of this secondary school there were 5 middle schools and 28 primary schools having bout 80 to 100 teachers.

The Commission felt that the clusters of these schools could become a fairly small and manageable group which can function in a face to face relationship within easily accessible distance. It has also a good potential for planning and guidance sincere there will be at least five or six trained graduates in the school—this group built around a secondary school should be adopted as a minimum viable unit of educational reform and develop accordingly.

The clustering suggested by the commission had first to be around the middle school with 8 to 10 primary schools on the basis of physical proximity. The headmaster of the middle school was to provide extension service to the component primary schools in his charge and to ensure smooth functioning of the primary schools. He was to head a committee of headmasters of the primary schools. The con.mittee was entrusted with the task of planning and development of all the schools as a part of a single complex. Then the middle schools falling in the area of influence of the secondary school constitute a higher level cluster. At this level, the headmaster of the secondary school will chair the committee consisting o headmasters of all the middle and primary schools.

Thus the headmaster of the secondary schools was to be the head of the school complex. The school complex committee would chalk out the plan, formulate academic calendar and give guidance to all the schools. It was envisaged that this group of schools and teachers could be given a good deal of freedom to develop their own programmes subject to general guidance of the inspecting staff. It should also be requested to coordinate its work with the local communities and to derive s much help from the source as possible.

The ideal behind the concept of school complex was to break the isolation in which each school functioned, to encourage cooperation among teachers to make the best use of resources, to decrease the load of inspecting staff and to leave education to the teachers and students. The commission visualized that the complex itself would perform certain delegated tasks which would otherwise have been performed by the inspecting officers of the department and dealt with individual schools within it. Under this programme, the school would gain its strength, would be able to exercise greater freedom, and help in making the system more elastic and dynamic. The department would also given. It would be able to concentrate its attention on major essentials and could afford to have fewer officers but at a high level of competence.

The scheme was tried as a pilot project in some states and soon was abandoned. No one has heard about it in recent years.

It was in 1966 again that the present author wrote a paper on spatial planning for rural development suggesting the of development of system of growth faci ranging from growth poles at the national level to growth centers at the micro level. Growth points at the local level and service centers at the micro-level where appropriate production and consumption functions could be clustered. The concept was quite similar to the idea of school complex, but was broader in content and coverage. This short paper with a germ of a theoretical frame work for spatial planning was elaborated later at the United Nations and published as a report in 1969. In the mean time, the Ford Foundation in India also developed a scheme of service centers for rural development. A more comprehensive version of the UN report was published as a book in 1974.

Spatial planners have used this framework for the

location of various social and economic activities in space. Computer progrmmes are now available for locational decisions. And some of the issues like threshold, accessibility can be easily resolved and hence we leave these issues here.

The question now is: even if the location of the school is most ideal, there is no guarantee that it would function well. We propose to take up this aspect of school planning. A village school can run well only if its three human components cooperate with each other and its infrastructure is well developed. The three human components are teachers, students and village community. Superimposed on this trinity are the institutions of the social system s a whole which can be termed as external factors. If the three internal elements do not function harmoniously and in cooperation with each other, not much can be achieved.

Now let us see where the school fits in present day scheme of development planning at the district, block mandal or village level. The fact of the matter is that school is outside the local planning process. Local and micro-level development means only rural development which essentially means agricultural and allied activities. Development, education and health are the activities of the line departments and a district or block development plan has no allocation for education.

As regards the role of Gram Panchayat, less said the better. School is not treated as an institution of the community. It is considered to be an activity of the government . Village do not feel shy of taking away school properties. Thefts are common. In many cases even doors and windows are taken away. The role of the teachers is equally frustrating. Absenteeism is too common. Teachers treating their teaching job a secondary or even tertiary is becoming a common phenomenon. The children who come to the school belong to illiterate families. Much of their time is spent in antic education environment. Unless there lack buildings, equipment, sports , etc. There is thus nothing that can enthuse village lads to attend schools.

Conclusion

What needs to be done? There is no lack of ideas and concepts. The school complex and growth center concepts are adequate tools to deal with some of the conventional problems. We need three major steps to restore to the village school the prestige it deserves. These are:

1. A movement to involve all concerned in school planning and development
2. A massive effort to mobilize resources for school infrastructure.
3. Self-regulation a envisaged in the school complex concept.

Unless the school becomes the hub of village activities and the whole community gets involved init, not much can be achieved. The above three measures also include incentives for school attendance. Spatial planning for school education should be linked with the concept of school complex to till gaps wherever they are.

Mobilization as stated earlier, means involvement of not only the local community but also the senior citizens, retired persons, students, educated youth and of course, the voluntary agencies. The task, to begin with should be target-oriented.

We can achieve full literacy among the people in the group of 5-40 within a period of five years if such a mobilization becomes a reality. The situation does not look as hopeless as a decade back. There is growing consciousness among the people to achieve something spectacular and to make this country moving again. What we lack today is the political will to rise above short-term and narrow ends, and a vision of new society that the Mahatma had in mind.

4

Responsive Administration and Panchayati Raj

Administrative system, responsive in the true sense of the terms, has to be conductive to the fulfillment of public needs and sensitive to public grievances. After independence the scope of administration continued of enlarge and it has had to shoulder new responsibilities and undertake tasks covering a wide spectrums of activities, ranging from planning and implementation of development. The focus of administration has shifted to building up 'the welfare state'. The task is no doubt being taken up but not to the expectations of downtrodden millions of this country. For them there appears to be no perceptible change—the same structure, the same norms, the same rule-oriented rigid office procedures and almost the same old outlook and attitude of public servants. They are unable to find any transformation, any revamping of the obsolete, rigid and static systems which seem to be persisting even after independence.

If the situation is analysed properly one comes to know that certain features of our present administrative system have been inherited from our colonial past. The British legacy emphasized 'command', the feelings of the 'subjects' were not of much consequence. It was, they thought, necessary for ensuring an orderly behaviour of the people. Administrative machinery was a sort of apparatus to dominate and oppress the Indians. The ghost of the mutiny of 1857 had always haunted the Britishers and they responded by establishing a highly centralized and unresponsive system of administration.

The most unfortunate part of this is that even after independence the same administrative structure, with all its traits, is continuing. Though the Britishers withdrew, the great leviathan, i.e. the machine of administration, remained intact not only as a manual of office -procedures, imposing physical buildings and functionaries, but also as established habits, prejudices interests and class barriers. There is hardly any departure from the past; innovations are few and far between. The bureaucracy which has been nurtured in the colonial and imperial tradition, exhibits traits of impersonality, compulsive professionalism and procedural rigidity.

It is not that the severity of the problem has not been realized or efforts not made to improve the situation. The greatest thrust on administrative reform at the national level came with the appointment of the Administrative Reforms Commission in 1966 which made a comprehensive study of administration at all levels. At the state level also a number of committees were appointed to suggest steps for improvement in administration. Among them could be mentioned Vellodi Committee (Kerala), Chandrakar Committee (Orissa),

Narsingh Rao Dixit Commission (M.P.), Hanumanthaiya Commission (Punjab), H.C. Mathur Committee (Rajasthan), S.G. Barve Committee (Maharashtra) A.D. Gorwala Report on Mysore Administration, Ramachandra Reddy Committee (Andhra Pradesh), Ashok Mitra Committee (West Bengal) and the Administrative Reforms Commission report on District Revenue and General Administration in Tamil Nadu.

There is a greater need today than ever before on the part of those who are planning for and manning administrative structures at various levels to conceptualize the real spirit of administration, which is infact a felt-need of the nation. They are obliged to reconcile responsiveness with other administrative values such as accountability and efficiency. The administration should be for the people and not people for the administration. The spirit is well reflected in the Indian Constitution also. A comparative picture of the objective, accountability, methods and functions of administration during pre and post-independence era may perhaps help I understanding the concept of responsive administration.

	Before 1947	*After 1947*
a. Main objective of the administrate system	To maintain British rule	Building up the welfare state
b. Accountable to	British Masters /Imperial set-up	i. Public ii. Constitution iii. Acts/Rules
c. Methods	Oppressive	Persuasive with constructive goals
d. Functions	Mainly regulatory	Both the regulatory and developmental but with greater

emphasis on the latter.

The world 'Responsive Administration' should not be confused with administrative reforms. Administrative reforms. No doubt, constitute a greater component of responsive administration. Responsive administration is in fact a state, a goal; while administrative reform is one of the means to achieve that goal. Neither can responsiveness be confused with responsibility or accountability. The two are administrative values only. Responsiveness in administration has a very wide scope. It is the total sum of all administrative values making the system capable of concentrating on public needs, removal of their grievances, rapid economic growth, extending to social reform, distributive justice and human resource development.

The realization of the objectives needs planning and today the focus of planning has shifted to grassroot i.e. planning form below. The district level plans which are aimed at the specific objectives of increasing production, reducing unemployment and eradicating poverty have to be so drawn that they get merged and integrated into state plan and later in turn into the national plan. The administrative system, therefore, has to be committed to the National level developmental objectives and for this purpose has to welcome people's participation at all the three levels—planning, decision making and implementation. In other words, the administrative system has to be not only responsible but also representative, accommodating active participation by the community.

"A truly responsive administration must hve two essential characteristics; it must be representative, and it must be responsible. At present, mst district administrations are not representative because we have allowed democratically elected local bodies to wither away . Even where elected local bodies do exist, planning and development functions are, to a large extent, divorced from these institutions. A district administration that is not a democratic administration cannot be a representative administration. A major systemic increase in responsiveness will arise out of making district administration more representative.

Such feelings of Rajiv Gandhi expressed in his inaugural address at the further Workshop of the District Magistrates and Collectors on 'Responsive administration' held at HCM Rajasthan State Institute of Public Administration, Jaipur, on April 30, 1988, were actually based on the conclusions which emerged from the earlier workshop held at Bhopa (December 10, 1987), Hyderabad, (February 13, 1988) and Imphas (April 2, 1988). This is an Indication of the fact that administrators working in different parts of the country also realized the necessity of people's representation in administration as one of the major steps towards making the administrative system more responsive. Some of the recommendations of the said workshops deserve attention.

i. Appropriate constitutional provisions for ensuring timely and regular elections to local democratic institutions.

ii. Decentralized district planning along with constitutional provision spelling out the subjects in the district sector.

iii. Restructuring of personnel polices and training programmes in the light of growing interface between administration and local bodies.

iv. Delegation of some functions of the government to local bodies and voluntary agencies.

The maintain responsiveness in administrative system a constant interaction between the public servants and the public is desirable. The supporters of public participation assert that it also enhances the effectiveness as well as responsiveness of the governmental policies and programmes sensitizing the public servants and their political superiors to probable consequences of their decisions. Thus people's participation is as important a responsible behaviour of public servants towards making the administration responsive.

People's participation in development administration and planning process becomes necessary:

a. To take note of the felt needs of the people
b. To mobilize local resources for implementation of schemes including people's labour
c. To anticipate and iron out possible conflicts or sharp differences at the planning and implementation stages
d. To expedite implementation of schemes by securing the cooperation of people
e. To increase the acceptance of the plan and projects and prgrammes underlying it; and
f. To bring bout a change in the power structure in people's institution in favour of the poor.

What should be the nature and extent of people's participation? It is neither easy nor desirable to suggest a uniform pattern for all parts of the world. In western countries literacy percentage is very high, people are quite conscious about their rights and duties as citizens, employment opportunities are sufficient, responsibilities relating to local level development are well taken care of by community and district councils and where rural areas are equally developed, the movement for people's participation has been very strong. There are various forms of participation viz., citizen groups, special interest groups, official citizen committees, speakers bureaus, consultations, survey and opinion polls etc.

Situation are however, quite different in India. Because of over population, scanty employment opportunities, low literacy percentage, legacies of colonial past, social customs, very large undeveloped rural areas and drought-flood affected agriculture, the people for almost all the days of year are busy fighting, with the poverty stricken situation and solving their problems relating to food, shelter and health. A vast majority of them are just docile human beings, what to talk of citizen's rights and duties, participation in the governmental programmes or two way communication with administrative machinery. These circumstances perhaps, led Balwantray Mehta Committee (1957) to suggest institutionalization of people's participation in the form of Panchayati Raj Institutions viz., Gram Panchayat, block Samiti and Zill Paraishad. Thus in the context of India, specially, rural India, giving shelter to 70 percent of population, it is proper to replace the world participation by representation.

When we talk of representative administration, it signifies that the administrative structure should represent the community also, the decision making be shared by the representatives of the public. The practical aspect of this concept is, if there are representatives from the lower strata of the society (i.e. weaker section) and the lowest unit of habitation (i.e. village) there is participation through democratic institutions (i.e.,

Panchayati Raj Institutions, Cooperative Societies and Voluntary Organizations, etc) at the local level, thus, becomes particularly important in the context of development administration. In a vast country like India with all its regional variation, it is vital that at the local level the enthusiasm and aspirations of the people are translated into con structure programmes of development through cooperative action.

In this context it is quite relevant, rather desirable, to examine the role, functioning and achievements of PRIs during the last 2-3 decades. There is a general feeling that these institutions suffer from elite domination and institutional ineffectiveness. Asoka Mehta Committee pointed out the emergence of the oligarchic politics in these bodies. However, it would be improper to say that PRIs have completely failed or have be no marked relevance in the affairs of rural development. These institutions have emerged as a ray of hope towards fulfilling local requirements and local participation in the process of planning and implementation. To a great extent these organs of democratic decentralization have been successful providing links between people and officials at the local level. With this, expectations of local people have raised to a certain level. A process of thinking has started within them abut their requirements a and role in the process of development. The role of official machinery too has been emphasized. On the other hand young leadership as a second line of representation has emerged in the rural areas. Being young, dynamic and aspirant for higher ladder, the office–bearers of PRIs, scattered allover the country, have successfully made the average citizen more conscious of his rights and thus helped in raising political consciousness of the people.

In this regard it is worth referring to the following observations of Askoa Mehta Committee (1977) "It will be wrong to think that Panchayati Raj should be viewed as a God that has failed. It has many achievements to its credit, the more important of which may be identified here. Politically speaking it became a process of democratic seed–drilling in the Indian soil, making an average citizen more conscious of his rights than before. Administratively speaking, it bridged the gulf between the bureaucratic elite and the people. Socio-culturally speaking it generated a new leadership which was not merely relatively young in age but also modernistic and pro-social change in outlook. Finally, locked at from the development angle, it helped rural people cultivate a developmental psyche.

The institutional ineffectiveness referred to can be observed from the performance of PRIs in certain functions aiming at improvements in the standard of primary education, village sanitation, family welfare, civil supplied, growth of agriculture production etc., to be more specific development schemes implemented through development department/DRDAs having objectives of increasing production, reducing unemployment and alleviating poverty. A number of programmes with one name or the other have been implemented for the development of rural poor. Intensive Agriculture District Programme (IADP), intensive Agriculture Area Programme (IAAP), High Yielding Varieties Programms (HYVP), Tribal Area Development Programme (TADP), Command Area Development programme (CADP), Antyodaya, Food for work (FFW), Integrated Rural Development Programme (IRDP), Training of Rural Youth for Self – Employment (TRYSEM), Development of Women and

Children in Rural Areas (DWCRA), National Rural Employment (RLEGP), Desert Development programme (DDP), Drought Prone Rea Prgromme for the poor though Minimum Needs Programme (MNP), Jawahar Rozgar Yojana (JRY) and many other such programmes are manifestations of the Government's concern for the cause of upliftment of rural masses. Most of them have been implemented through PRIs. Thousand of crores of rupees have been spent in each five year Plan for the cause of rural development. Yet the basic problems of poverty, unemployment and underemployment, income inequalities, regional disparities, etc. are still there. There should be no hitch in admitting the fact that there are so many areas where nether the beneficiaries fell satisfied ad hopeful nor the planners and executors are convinced, infact, the sense of achievement is not there. Rural development should aim not only at a higher growth rate or more output but also at proper distribution of the gains of growth and assurance of socio–economic justice.

Who is to be blamed? Panchayati Raj Institutions, bureaucracy, administrative systems or public? Having no intentions to minimize the responsibility of PRIs for not achieving the real objectives (not merely the targets) there are certain aspects which deserve to be looked into.

1. An Examination of the development programmmes, implemented so far for the betterment of life areas indicates two things.

a. Most of the programmes had been designed in such a way that their implementation was found to be on uniform pattern throughout the country.

b. Decision making was restricted to either the central or the state government.

This situation caused inherent weaknesses in the planning of these schemes; many aspects could not be reflected to the desired extent. To be more specific local needs, local resources and local participation were not appreciated properly in the centralized planning. In a country like India where regional and sub-regional disparities and contrasts are so deep, fertility and production levels are so varying and per capita income and consumption are so different even within a smaller area that no uniform pattern can be practicable and fruitful. In a centralized plan for a country of the size of India it is impossible to keep the requirements of all regions, sub-regions and further smaller units in view. And without proper perception of actual requirements a development scheme cannot prove meaningful.

To cite an example, IRDP is an investment programme, being implemented throughout the country with a view to alleviate poverty by raising income through increased production and creating opportunities for self employment. Certain items such as milch–cow, camel cart, bullock cart, sheep and goal have been prescribed as suitable assets to be provided to the beneficiaries i.e, persons below poverty line. The scheme is being implemented with the same norms in different parts of the country, whether it is tribal belt of Madhya Pradesh or fertile tracts of Punjab or Haryana. Certainly the level of economic attainment and accordingly the requirements of the farmers of Punjab and tribals of Jagdalpur Bastar area are altogether different. There are many districts in Western U.P., Haryana, Punjab and in some other parts of the country where it is difficult to trace out the persons below poverty line. But IRDP is there, targets are there. Needless to mention, with the same investment a different scheme based on local requirements could be formulated. And such a scheme would have proved fruitful in real sense. It can certainly be possible through decentralized (district) planning.

2. Lack of proper linkage between development schemes and infrastructure has been another weak aspect of our planning. What to talk of infrastructure to be created, even the existing infrastructure has not been used properly. It is perhaps because of the sectoral approach for formulation of schemes. Unless the concept of integrated area planning which is akin to the concept of district (Decentralized) planning is adopted, establishment of backward and forward linkage cannot be taken as a very important aspect of a development scheme. For instance, no diary development programme can succeed without a net of rural roads, milk collection centers, marketing facilities, chilling plants, proper supply of fodder, veterinary hospitals, semen banks and proper training etc.

3. As such the development schemes along with the methodology for implementation are just imposed upon PRIs from above. They are not in a position to make any decision regarding any aspect of the scheme.

4. As far as implementation of development schemes is concerned it has a funnel-shaped form, having so many agencies at apex (i.e., DRDA, Zilla Parishad, Collector, Development department, special schemes organization, and many other departments engaged in rural development) and only one agency (Panchayat Samiti or Mandal) at the base. Ironically, all these agencies working at apex level have no coordination among themselves. Each of them expects priority for its scheme at the implementation level. i.e.

Panchayat Samiti or Madal. Such a situation not only disturbs the time calendar but also creates some practical problems (caused by ego of senior officers) for the officials working at implementation level.

5. It is a general feeling that the powers given to PRIs are just on papers. Neither proper infrastructure nor sufficient funds are there to execute the powers. Many office-bearers of these institutions have been heard saying that the will of state governments is altogether missing as far as real strengthening of PRIs is concerned.

6. Some of the provisions of acts and rules framed to run the PRIs involve practical difficulties regarding heir application, specially those which are meant to regulate the powers and duties of officials vs public representatives.

7. Mostly the staff posted in PRIs are on deputation from other departments such as agriculture, cooperative societies, education, social welfare industries. It has been observed that such borrowed staff are neither loyal to their new controlling officers nor committed to he philosophy of Panchayati Raj.

8. Many of the administrative officers posted in PRIs re not development minded. In fact, they do not want to shed their elitist approach to become rural – oriented. Such officers find themselves unable to seek full cooperation of non-officials, voluntary organizations and public representatives.

9. Looking into the extent of field work and required mobility, PRIs, specifically the Panchayat Samitis and Mandals, have insufficient transport facilities. This badly affects monitoring of development schemes.

10. In spite of all the drawback and limitations the PRIs have successfully provided organizational infrastructure at the local level throughout the country which could set in motion development programmes and bring about a change in the power structure of people's institutions in favour of the rural peasantry. It has been observed that many a work, specially the pucca works taken up under NREP and RLEGP programmes have been completed by these institutions efficiently, well within time and at a comparatively cheaper rate.

11. There has been a relative cooling-off' of enthusiasm of Members of Parliament, Members of State Legislative Assemblies and others towards Pnachayti Raj, as they perceived a lurking threat to their leadership in the emerging Panchayati Raj. An unexpressed feeling is always there that the Zilla Pramukhs and Block Pradhans, having sufficient funds, development schemes, infrastructure and machinery, are certainly in a better position as far as extending influence in the area is concerned. This has caused undesirable rivalry between MLAs and Block Pradhas Officials working in the block samitis are invariably victims of such rivalry. Whatever decision an officer takes it has to go infavour of one side (or it is assumed like this). This situation not only disturbs mental peace of the officer concerned but also has an adverse effect on the implementation of development schemes.

12. It would not be out of place to mention that wherever, state governments have taken up determined efforts to strengthen Panchayti Raj, the PRIs in those states, in spite of political and bureaucratic resistance at initial stage, have started functioning and achieving the objectives successfully. People, in these sates, also

have absorbed this message. Karnataka, Gujarat and West Bengal are some examples. Though following different patterns PRIs in these states have made their own place in the affairs of local administration.

a. Karnataka. As far as democratic decentralization and people's participation in the planning process are concerned, Karnataka can boast to be the most progressive and forward looking state. With the enanctment of The Karnataka Zilla Parishad and Mandal Panchayart Act in 1985 and its enforcement in March 1987 a new chapter ha been added to the administrative history of Karnataka. The act which basically follows the model suggested by the Asoka Mehta Committee (1977) gives the highest priority to rural development through democratic decentralization and need –based local planning. It aims at alround improvement in the economy through people's participation. To strengthen PRIs financially the state government ha decided to transfer 40 percent of the plan expenditure and 50 percent of non-plan expenditure to Zilla Parishads for implementing district secror schemes. Regarding function of PRIs in the new set-up some extracts from the report of the Zilla Parishad and Mandal Panchayat Evalaution committee, March 1989 are worth referring to. The report mentions that:

"Despite all limitations, the actual achievements of Zilla Parishads and Mandal Panchayats are impressive. Virtually in all districts; the operation of schools and health facilities has improved vastly. Attendance of both, teacher and students, has gone up noticeably. Priority has been given to the extension, repairs and maintenance of school buildings.

There has been significant progress In the area of

medical stores purchase policy, and Zilla Parishads have been able to secure more of their supplies locally, more cheaply and promptly.

"Considerable progress has also been made in the allocation of housing sites under Janata and other special housing schemes. For construction of houses under low income housing programmes, efforts have been made to utilize local resources, in spite of pressures to entrust these works to outside organization.

"A major achievement of these institutions (PRIs) is the systematic development of inland fisheries".

"Public servants are more conscious of their accountability not just to their superiors in office but to the people of whose government they are employees.

B. Gujarat. A three–tier system of Panchayati Raj has been functioning in Gujarat since 1963 but in the wake of thrust for decentralized planning the system is passing through the stage of revitalization. Unlike Karnataka a separate body 'District Planning Board' has been constituted to undertake planning functions. However, the Panchayati Raj Institutions are associated wit the planning boards very closely. The PRIs have been assigned a vast field of development along with functions. Powers and resources a their command. All the programmes relating to Community Development, Agriculture, Irrigation, Animal Husbandry, Cooperation, Education, Social Education, Health and Sanitation, Family Welfare, Women and Child Health programme. Social welfare housing communication, Tribal Welfare and many other allied programmes have been transferred and entrusted to the Panchayats. Certain revenue and other regulatory functions have also been assigned to them. Rescue operations and relief measures at the time of natural calamities like flood, fire, cyclone, earthquake are also carried out by the Panchayat administration successfully. Presently numerous plan and non-plan schemes of different departments including the schemes under 15 percent discretionary and 5 percent incentive outlay of District Planning Boards and also the schemes of tribal area sub-plan are formulated and implemented by the PRIs. In a nutshell, acceptance of Panchayati raj system by people in the rural areas of Gujarat is in itself and indication of its relevance in the present administrative structure.

c. West Bengal. West Bengal is the state where political, social and economic culture of the rural community is changing very fast because of the strengthening of Panchayati Raj system. With a very strong 'political will at the state level PRIs have become really effective and meaningful as far as people's participation in local administration and planning for rural development is concerned. Sabhadhipati, the chairman of Zilla Parishad is also the Chairman of District Planning committee, DRDA and so many other district level committee which were earlier headed by the Collector. The Collector is the executive officer of Zilla Parishad.

Public pressure through PRI and party cadre of CPI(M) is so strong here that the district administration is inclined to be conductive to the public needs. Like wise the planning also reflects the local requirements on priority basis. Whether registration of share croppers selection of IRDP beneficiaries, works under JRY or preparing local plans, in every sphere of local administration PRIs have an effective say. The most remarkable feature is that with the changing political, social and economic culture the value system of the office-bearers of PRIs is also changing under the public pressure. Thus most of their decisions now are fairly objective.

It is often stated by people both in government and outside that Panchayati Raj Institutions suffer from elite domination i.e. domination of upper castes, richer people or other entrenched interests in rural society. It may be true to some extent but it us also true that such domination is getting minimized year by year by invisible pressure of community. Take the case of west Bengal where the grip of Bhada lokas' is loosing strength; gram Panchayats, by and large, now are represented by *Chhot lokas*. With the increasing awareness in rural masses on account of education, communication and changing patterns of economy the percentage of such domination is bound to reduce. During the last general election to Lok Sabha (1991 May-June) the defact of some rules, who were virtually worshipped in their respective areas, proves this hypothesis. It should not be forgotten that elected functionaries of PRIs are always subject to effective surveillance by their electors. What is required to cure the disease of elite domination is to regulate the elections under some mandatory provisions and strengthen PRIs function and resource-wise. Regularity and method of elections world to a large extent determine the type of persons elected. The committee constituted to evaluate the functioning of Zilla Prishads and Mandal Panchayats of Karnataka found the caliber of men and women elected to these offices remarkably high.

To enhance the sense of responsibility among the office-bearers of PRIs, elections may be held on party-basis. With political parties in tray the advantage would be that in view of the direct and continuous accountability of the elected to the elector at this level, the parties would try and sponsor responsible persons as a candidates. In any case, even is political parties were responsible persons as candidates. In any case, even if political parities were formally excluded, they would still remain behind the scene and extend their support to one or the other of candidates. By associating political parties formally the process would be more open and transparent. The local elections on party line would also be the training ground for candidates who get elected to take on responsibilities at higher levels later, the state and the center.

So often corruption and misuse of position by office-bearers of PRIs is talked of. They are not the exceptions, nor is the percentage of persons unusual. If there is something exceptional or unusual, it is their escape, many a time, from the orbit of disciplinary action under relevant Act. Needless to mention, lack of systems, undue long and rigid procedures and their out of administrative system position help them in getting rid of. Once if they are made part of representative and responsible administrative system it would be difficult for them to work in irresponsible and undesirable manner. Of course, there are some areas which deserve immediate attention in regard to proper functioning of PRIs. A deep analysis and action research is warranted on the issues such as decision making process in PRIs, implementation of decisions office administration, accountability and inter- relationship between official and non-official office–bearers of PRIS.

To conclude, responsible administration, symbolically, is a tripod structure which is based, to a large extent, on democratic decentralization decentralized planning process and responsible behaviour of the public servants.

Panchayati Raj Institutions, district planning and administrative reforms are the practical manifestations of these. In this regard, Constitution (64th Amendment) Bill Presented by Rajv Gñdhi in the Lok Sabha on May 15, 1989 was an important step towards making the these local bodies really purposeful, active, self-supporting and effective. It is good that the present government too has positive attitude on the issue.

On August 6, 1991 addressing the All India Constructive Workers Conference the Prime Minister

Shri. P.V. Narsimha Rao pledged that his government would provide a legal framework to the syetem of democratic decentralization as envisaged by the Panchayati Raj System. That he would set right the distortions of history and evolve a viable system of Panchayati Raj system through law and through consensus. The lack of coordination between field workers and the policy makers in Delhi has to be rectified. Et us hope for the best. One thing is certain, if once it is materialized it would be a turning point in he history of Panchayati Raj and Rural Development.

5

Reflections on Panchayati Raj

Since ancient times, rural India had development democratic tractions. The main objective was to promote economic development with distributive justice. The people formed little republics to function as a unit. It was called a Samiti. In which all the village elders discussed the issues pertaining to the village. It can be compared to the present day gram samba, during Vedic times each village elders got together to discuss local issues and the venue was called choral participation in the meeting was considered as a privilege. During the latter part of the Vedic period, they had put an end to Gram Sabha system as bigger kingdoms emerged.

The powers and functions were with the king and all the issues were discussed in the *darbar*. This led to centralization of power and subsequently village republics lost importance.

In Gupta era, two concepts received importance " *(i)* feudalism and *(ii)* castes. These factors promoted imperialism and the village level the rich dominant castes acquired power. The rich formed trade guilds (Mahajans) and Nadu (Group) in south, on the basis of caste. After fifteenth century PR institutions became weak, religious and caste base gained importance the reason being Muslim invasion and their military power and due to certain disturbances in India. Subsequently Muslim rulers did not take interest in such actives like Panchayats or unions or local self-government and they did not evince interest, but were collecting revenue. Delhi was ruled by Muslim but in far flung areas groups of people managed those regions by way of Samantas. And Jamindars. However at the village level, the rich landlord commanded the people for personal gains.

When the Britishers entered India, the situation was as mentioned above, which was far from the ancient Panchayat system of Vedic period. The inordinate greed of the East India company caused slow but steady disintegration of these village Panchayats. They introduced Landlordism and the Ryotwari system as against the MAUZWARI of village tenure system giving severe blow to the corporate life of the village tenure system giving severe blow to the corporate life of the village tenure system giving severe blow to the corporate life of the village communities. The British rulers did not the greatest disservice to our country by destroying the ancient traditional village Panchayats and trying to replace them by their officers whose sole interest was to please the alien rulers by exploiting the people of the India to a great extent.

In 1935 local self-government was enacted by the government, in which some of the activities were transferred and handed over to the local authorities. However, they remained on paper as the Second World War stated in 1936. Some efforts were made to revive

Panchayats in 1920 by passing the Bombay village Panchayat Act, wherein powers were given to the collectors of the District local Board. In this Act, three important factors were introduced: *(1)* voting rights to adults, *(2)* elected members of the village Panchayat, and *(3)* the control was given to the Collectors or the District Local Board. These efforts were not appreciated and on the whole the working of these institutions was far from satisfactory.

After independence, it was development through bureaucratic set-up. The major challenge for the system, therefore, comes from the presence of the skewed class structure. In other words, there are unprecedented inequalities of wealth and power. In a society based on poverty, inequality and immobility and gross disparities, consensus would mean the interest of the dominant class. The official component of administration failed to understand the needs of the people at large. Society is a broader concept than the State and it encompasses not only power relations but also a variety of symbolic, regulating and other relations and individuals and groups. The administrative set-up, with its own terms and conditions guaranteed under the constitution, retained the structure and style of its elitist nature. Hence, it is perpetuating the national administrative system, based on the colonial functions of law and order than undertaking broad responsibilities for socio-economic development. The administrative ethos have suffered very little change during the last 3-4 decades. General observations tend to support strongly the view that, although there has been much discussion about the development of a more democratic administrative style, there has been little change in actual practice. It is also pointed out that among the variables impeding effective implementation, perhaps the most significant is the bureaucratic machinery, failed to translate planned goals into action. The Consitution adopted in 1950 considered the citizen of India as an important component of the democratic set-up. Greater thrust was given to the attainment of a socialistic pattern of the society. The development of villages remained an important item in the agenda of planned documents.

Deficiencies of the Government are seen as: *(1)* Powers derived from above, *(2)* Bureaucracy working as per instructions laid down and, therefore, there are least chances for deviating from guidelines to meet the local needs, *(3)* Target oriented, i.e., only working within the frame-work and not beyond, *(4)* Hardly localized and, therefore, failure to bring about required development, *(5)* It does provide sufficient resources to fulfill the requirements of the programme, *(6)* Finance derived from above on the basis of target fulfillment and scheme without proper identification of beneficiary and the local need.

Review of Rural Development

Rural development is important for India, likewise other goals such as nation building, economic growth and social progress and, therefore, we need definite approaches and strategies to bring about new changes in development. Earlier, the development was identified with growth in gross national product or economic growth. But, with conceptual changes in regard to socio-economic progress, it is viewed from a rather different perspective. We must take into account economic growth along with socio-cultural and politico-administrative contexts.

In order to fulfill the felt-needs of the rural weaker sections, efforts have been made through generation of economic opportunities and by providing better welfare facilities.

The development process is and 'action-oriented administrative system'. The basic assumption that the desired change could be ushered in rural areas with the help of an administrative machinery capable of providing infrastructural facilities and technical know-how has failed to catch and deliver the goods. There was least participation of people's representatives. The observations regarding inadequacies and limitations of administrative system can be listed.

1. Conceived in administrative terms, it remained a bureaucratic activity where the officials were 'target oriented', and showed little sensitivity to the social process generated by economic programmes, people's participation was substituted by bureaucratic mobilization directed towards achieving set goals of development.
2. Development programmes were not conceived in response to the 'felt-needs' of the people. It obviously implieu that participation was lacking in determining development priorities. Unfortunately, 'felt-need' as the basis of the programme of the local community remained merely a slogan as the officials were not even familiar with the methods of ascertaining these needs.
3. The human and material resources were most inadequate considering the scale and magnitude of the task that was to be accomplished.
4. What was supposed to be a 'people's

programme', had probably little or no say at all in either determining development priorities or the strategies for implementing the same. In the minor role of supporting and endorsing the programme designed for their development, the people could not forge new working relationships, with the bureaucrats.

The experience of CDP and the NES has pointed out that these schemes lacked the qualitative thrust while implementing the programmes.

Therefore, the idea of 'a set of institutional arrangements' was conceived during the First Five Year Plan and plan document stated that "so long as local self-government institutions are not concerned as parts of the same organic constitutional and administrative framework, the structure of democratic government will remain incomplete".

The phenomenon of government administration is based on hierarchy, power control, rigidity, sub ordinationism and unity and command which directly or indirectly influenced the low rate of development. In every modern state the ever-increasing role of administration has focused attention on the urgent need for unity in administrative process. Conflicts, bottlenecks, deadlocks, and break-downs in administrative mechanism are not infrequent. Integration and coordination have, therefore, become a sine qua non of a good administrative system today.

After examining the shortfall of the administrative arrangements it is felt essential that an alternative arrangement is necessary to govern out country to bring out rural development which is important in the context of socio-economic development. The decentralized powers and resources to districts and blocks, and if necessary to the grassroots, was envisaged by Balwantray Mehta Committee (1957) which recommended the strategy of decentralizing power, resources and functions to the local institutions as those institutions can act as the true representatives of rural India.

The Mehta committee observed that failure of the CDP a was due to the conspicuous absence of people's participation. In order to streamine this, the committee suggested that a set of institutional arrangements would have to be created to make participation meaningful and effective. Thus, began an experiment in the sphere of rural development administration to formulate and execute development programmes through people's participation meaningful and effective. Thus, began an experiment in the sphere of rural development administration to formulate and execute development programme through people's participation.

1. There should be three-tier structure of local self–governing bodies from village to district levels, with an organic link from the lower to the higher ones:
2. There should be genuine transfer of power and responsibilities to these bodies.
3. Adequate financial resources should be transferred to these bodies to enable them to discharge these responsibility.
4. All Development programmes at these levels should be channelled through these bodies ; and

The nature and content of decentralization includes democratic decentralization; structural decentralization; decentralization of planning at the grassroot level;

decision-making; delegation of powers; it should be through local institution; and it should not be used as a mechanical device but based on humanitarian aspects.

Advantages. Decentralisation has many advantages. In the first place, it removes the danger of "apoplexy at the top and anemia at the extremities." The dispersal of authority, functions and responsibility, on the one hand, brings relief to the overburdened central authority, and strengthens field agencies and grassroot units, on the other. Secondly, the people immediately affected get an opportunity for adaptation and adjustment in the administrative programmes and operations which are brought closer to them. Thirdly, dispersal of authority encourages faster action, reduces delays and shortens the red-tapism. Overall efficiency of administration, thus increases. Fourthly, it gives an opportunity to develop resourcefulness and self-respect among subordinate administrators, who thus have to fend for themselves, to take their own decisions, and shoulder their own responsibilities. Fifthly, decentralization facilitates experiments by various units by not committing the entire organization to particular course of action. It also permits health competition among units. Lastly, decentralization has more important justification than mere administrative efficiency. It bears directly upon the development of a sense of personal adequacy in the individual citizen; it has spiritual connotations. There are demerits also, but they are outweighed by the aforesaid merits to bring out social goals.

In this system four factors are relevant: responsibility, administrative, functional and external. Responsibility and administrative factors are interrelated and authority and responsibility go hand in hand, and so long as the central authority is responsible for any action. The main operational factors may be the variety of functions, which can be easily decentralized at the appropriate lowest levels. The external factors may include the demand for popular participation in programmes and the pressure of political parties.

Constitutional framework. The constitution framers, rather than making any effort to clean up this mess handed over responsibility to the states. Article 40 in the Directive principles instructed the state to transfer such powers and authority as might be necessary to enable panchayats to function as units of self–government. Similarly, the pattern of District Administration continues with the Directive principle (Article50). As a result, the system did not take the shape as it was desired except in few states.

On the basis of Balwantray Mehta Committee Report, Rajasthan and Andhra Pradesh were the first two states to implement most of the recommendations and thereby broadly accepting the pattern suggested by the states can be broadly clubbed with one of these two. Although Magarashtra and Gujarat followed the broad pattern suggested by the Mehta committee, they made the Zilla Parishad the most important of the three tiers. They also introduced direct elections. Further they appointed a chief executive officer of the rank of District collector and also placed the district level technical and non-technical heads of branches under Zilla Parishad.

It is difficult to sum up the characteristics of the PRIs in all states in the country. The essential features of most of them revolve round the number of tiers, the mode of election, association of MLAs and MPs with these bodies, committee system, bureaucracy, finances and the relation of these bodies with the state government. At present the PRIs and leaders feel that they do not have enough autonomy. What is even more discomforting to the advocates of autonomy is the finding that the leadership of the more active blocks in terms of adopting new techniques of social and economic development tends to feel more strongly than others that their local government lacks power and that they should depend on the higher echelons of government to do development job. With all its defects the very fact that the leaders have to approach the people and to be in close touch with them has certainly sowed the seeds greater democratic participation. Consequently PR has tended to make rural politics a more continuous occupation, as local political leaders have stared mobilizing voters not only for the occasional election to a far removed legislative body but also to a hare in the day-to-day Panchayat decisions and development problems affecting their constituents. Panchayat leaders have gained importance as one of the major props which MLAs have for their elective and political support.

As a result, the decision making power in the local political System has also shifted significantly. Formerly, the decisions about the development of the district was taken at the state level by ministers and bureaucrats having a strong urban background. These were implemented by an impersonal administration lacking in development consciousness. With the introduction of PR, the decisions are taken by representatives of the rural masses at the district and the lower levels. These new decision makers are firmly rooted in rural setting and are sufficiently conscious of the developmental needs of their areas.

Mass movement. If we want to achieve the goal properly, it is quite essential that the people must be motivated, and peoples involvement in development is the only answer to this. Who can do this job? The answer is that the PRIs can only play an effective role of motivation. Mahatma Gandhi could succeed in freedom movement only on mass movement based on the swadeshi goods and the Khadi. Likewise, the rural development can succeed if it is based on peoples involvement in providing local answers to local needs.

In order to justify these observation, it would be proper to present the results of an interesting study in two different districts, viz., surat in Gujarat, where PR is in existence, and in Dhenkanal district of Orison, where PR is not in operation on the pattern of Gujarat.

It can be seen from the above facts that sutra district is far ahead in satisfaction of development rather than Dhenkanal district in Orison. Further, in surat district the socio-economic structure curve shows a pattern of high

Upward direction whereas in Dhenkanal District, it shows a slow upward direction. It can be directly attributed to the people's participation through the PRIs.

Sl.No.	*Item*	*Surat*	*Dhenkanal*
1.	Individual level of satisfaction with development benefits (%) Total satisfaction	3.2	1.9
2.	Satisfaction with present Financial condition (%)	12.9	4.3
3.	Level of overall satisfaction with development (%)	22.5	7.2
4.	Overall satisfaction with development perception of village problems	124.0	33.0
5.	Overall satisfaction with development with solution to village problem (High rate)	117.0	32.0

Panchayati Raj and Poor. The rural poor at times are unable to utilize special programmes due to governmental policy. One such instance is popular contribution. In certain cases rural poor are not in a position to contribute to the success of the programme. For e.g., in Gujarat, the housing programme for landless people can only be executed provided Rs. 500 is contributed by the District Panchayat. Without that amount the remaining Rs. 9500 will not reach the beneficiary.

Surat district Panchayat did excellent job in social forestry. The members promoted 40 primary societies. It had won both national and state awards. Another major breakthrough was in promoting five sugar factories with more than one lakh membership exclusively from the poor and oppressed sections of the society.

Surat district Panchayat was able to get some funds from the Zilla Parishad with a condition to reimburse when grants are received from the government. Thus, about 20 PHCs will start functioning from March 1992.

While concluding, it is essential to state that the existing differences in the socio-economic milieu can be reduced only through local bodies where popular participation is possible with less bureaucratic interference.

LOCAL CAPACITY FOR IMPLEMENTATION OF RURAL DEVELOPMENT PROGRAMMES (THE CASE OF WEST BENGAL AND BIHAR)

One of the basic principles of democracy is that decisions shall be made by those who are affected by them. This has given rise to the conviction that today's population of democratic institutions constituted by them alone are competent to judge what decisions are the right ones and suitable to them. It is generally accepted that genuine local governments have a potential for promoting socio-economic development in various ways. Some important aspects are:

i) It facilitates inculcation of positive attitudes by citizens, such as consideration, self-control, community responsibility and identity;

ii) Provision of basic community services which improve the quality of people's lives and enable the community to generate and attract economic activities;

iii) Helping people, especially in the rural areas, to organise them-selves for the mobilization and effective management of community resources and central government programmes respectively.

Unfortunately eventhough India has embarked on decentralization programmes in view of these realizations, the overall effect of such efforts have simply come to mean, in majority of States, continuing support of deconcentrated bureaucracy rather than an effective system of local self-government.

This paper argues that local self-government in the shape of Panchayati Raj Institutions (PRIs) is capable of taking up responsibility of poverty alleviation and rural development programmes provided they are allowed to build local capacity. Local capacity symbolises the ability of the people to articulate their needs and to identify actions to solve them. It also represents the ability of the people to mobilize and organise local or extra-local resources in the pursuit of communally defined goals.

Methodology

The present paper is based on a larger study conducted in two major states, namely, West Bengal and Bihar. In the PR Institutions are responsible for executing rural development programmes while in the latter, the responsibilities devoted on them are limited in nature. The study was to gather perceptions about PR bodies as organizational structures to Take up the onerous task of promoting rural development. Two types of respondents were contacted: officials and non-officials. The officials were drawn from every level of hierarchy i.e., State, District., Block and Gram Panchayat (including PR bodies) who are, by and large, involved in the implementation of rural development programmes. The other segment of respondents were non-official members (elected/nominated or coopted) of PR bodies at the three levels. The sample size of official respondents were 25 from West Bengal and 30 from Bihar; whereas, the non-officials were 25 each from the states of West Bengal and Bihar. Each category of respondents were selected randomly for the purpose and a structured schedule was canvassed. Apart from that discussions were also held on the various items with them.

Perception About Panchayati Raj

The response pattern showed a positive commitment to PRIs being involved in the implementation of rural development programmes.

Table 1: Should PRIs be Involved in the Implementation of Rural Development Programmes (Officials)

S.No.	*Response*	*Bihar*	*West Bengal*
1.	Yes	21(70.0)	25(100.0)
2.	No	9(30.0)	--
	Total	30(100.0)	25(100.0)

The unanimous positive pesponse of all the respondents from West Bengal may be due to the fact that the PR system has taken deep roots in West Bengal and the bureaucracy has, over a period of time, adjusted itself to the situation.

The officials were probed through an open-ended question: who is their opinion should be responsible for the implementation of rural development programmes? The response was divided: While some of them preferred the machinery of the sectoral departments, others preferred PR Institutions. None, however, mentioned the name of the District Rural Development Agency (DRDA) to implement these programmes. The response pattern is presented in Table 2.

Table 2: Agency that Should Implement Rural Development Programmess (Officials)

S.No.	*Response*	*Bihar*	*West Bengal*
1.	Panchayati Raj	25(83.3)	19(76.0)
2.	DRDA	--	--
3.	Department Concerned	5(16.7)	1(4.0)
10.	NR/DK	--	5(20.0)
	Total	30(100.0)	25(100.0)

An analysis of the foregoing two Tables brings out an interesting feature that when confronted with an open-ended question, the response in favour of PR bodies as implementing agency came down from 100 to 76 per cent in West Bengal whereas in Bihar it registered an increase from 70 to 83 per cent. This would seem to show that even in the minds of officials the primacy of PR as the indispensable agency to plan and implement rural development schemes has not take unequivocal position.

Table 3 gives data about programmes that are being implemented by PR bodies. The non-official respondents from West Bengal were fully aware of the importance of local institutions and thus were better placed in identifying various categories of rural development programmes being implemented by these bodies. In Bihar, the response of the non-officials showed that the PR bodies are involved only in a limited way with regard to implementation of IRD Programmes and that, in general, no other category of rural development progamme is being implemented through these bodies.

Table 3: Programes/Schemes being implemented by Panchayati Raj Institutions (Non-Officials)

S.No.	*Response*	*Bihar*	*West Bengal*
1.	NREP	--	14(56.0)
2.	Several Programmes like Rural Water Supply	--	9(36.0)
3.	IRDP	2(8.0)	2(8.0)
4.	No scheme is implemented	23(92.0)	--
	Total	100(100.0)	25(100.0)

When the non-officials were further probed as to

what development schemes they would suggest for implementation by PR Institutions, 40 per cent of the respondents from Bihar and 44 per cent from West Bengal suggested that employment generation programmes like NREP/RLEGP should be implemented by the PR bodies. Regarding other schemes, the remaining respondents from both the states said that "all" the rural development programmes should be entrusted to these bodies.

Thus, both from the bureaucracy and from people's representatives, a very large number favoured Panchayati Raj bodies to deal with the development of rural areas.

Whenever rural development programmes are sought to be entrusted to PR bodies, the question of their administrative inefficiency is generally raised. To test the legitimacy of the same, we sought the views of the official and non-official respondents. Their response pattern is indicated in Table 4.

Table 4: Views About Administrative Inefficiency in Panchayati Raj

S.No.	*Response*	*Bihar*		*West Bengal*	
		Official	*Non-Official*	*Official*	*Non-Official*
1.	Strongly Agree	8 (26.7)	4 (16.0)	- -	- -
2.	Agree	15 (60.0)	15 (50.0)	5 (20.0)	11 (44.0)
3.	Disagree	7 (16.0)	4 (23.0)	11 (60.0)	4 (16.0)
4.	Strongly Disagree	-	2 (8.2)	5 (20.0)	10 (40.0)
	Total	30 (100.0)	25 (100.0)	25 (100.0)	25 (100.0)

Eventhough PR has taken roots in West Bengal, 20 per cent of official and 44 per cent of non-official respondents were or the view that administrative inefficiency is prevalent in PR bodies. Despite the preponderance of disagreement with the question, there would seem to be room for much improvement in the area of administrative efficiency. On the other hand in Bihar, where PR system has not taken firm roots, 76 per cent each of official and non-official respondents agreed about administrative inefficiency. It is, thus, clear that the administrative efficiency of the PR bodies needs toning up.

Administrative inefficiency could be the consequence of several reasons such as inadequacy of staff, their frequent transfer, lack of coordination, shortage of funds, shortage of material. Accordingly, the extent of their contribution to administrative inefficiency was gone into. The responses of the official and non-official respondents about their perception of the contributing factors to the administrative inefficiency are given in the Tables 5 to 10.

Table 5: Inadequacy of Staff for Implementing the Programme

S.No.	*Response*	*Bihar*		*West Bengal*	
		Official	*Non-Official*	*Official*	*Non-Official*
1.	Yes	14 (46.7)	20 (80.0)	1 (4.0)	3 (12.0)
2.	No	16 (53.3)	3 (12.0)	24 (96.0)	22 (88.0)
3.	NR/DK	--	2(8.0)	--	--
	Total	30 (100.0)	25 (100.0)	25 (100.0)	25 (100.0)

In West Bengal, thanks to the more-than-a-decade existence of PRIs, inadequacy of staff has not been perceived as a problem by 96 per cent of officials and 88 per cent of non-officials; whereas, in Bihar, 46.7 per cent officials and 80 per cent of non-officials have perceived this as a factor contributing to administrative inefficiency.

Table 6: Inefficiency of Staff

S.No.	*Response*	*Bihar*		*West Bengal*	
		Official	*Non-Official*	*Official*	*Non-Official*
1.	Yes	12(40.0)	10(40.0)	16(64.0)	18(72.0)
2.	No	18(60.0)	15(60.0)	9(36.0)	7(28.0)
	Total	30(100.0)	25(100.0)	25(100.0)	25(100)

In West Bengal, the majority of respondents, officials and non-officials, have perceived the staff to be inefficient while, in Bihar, it is not so. The PR bodies do not have their own staff. Their staff are mostly state government employees working with them. During the discussions, both the officials and non-officials expressed the view that many of the employees lack motivation and a sense of commitment to their work and when an occasion arises; till then, they are content to treat their present assignment in PR bodies as a transit posting. Where the staff members have been directly recruited by the PR bodies from the open market many of them are not effective or efficient because of the perceived absence of opportunities for career advancement.

Table 7: Frequency of Transfer of Staff

S.No.	Response	Bihar		West Bengal	
		Official	*Non-Official*	*Official*	*Non-Official*
1.	Yes	18 (60.0)	11 (44.0)	4 (16.0)	6 (24.0)
2.	No	11 (36.7)	8 (32.0)	21 (84.0)	19 (76.0)
3.	NR/DK	1 (3.3)	6 (24.0)	--	--
	Total	30 (100.0)	25 (100.0)	25 (100.0)	25 (100.0)

As can be made out from Table 7, resorting to frequent transfer of staff has been perceived as a contributing factor for inefficiency mainly in Bihar.

Table 8: Lack of Coordination

S.No.	Response	Bihar		West Bengal	
		Official	*Non-Official*	*Official*	*Non-Official*
1.	Yes	24 (80.0)	14 (56.0)	12 (48.0)	9 (36.0)
2.	No	6 (20.0)	11 (44.0)	13 (52.0)	16 (64.0)
	Total	30 (100.0)	25 (100.0)	25 (100.0)	25 (100.0)

At the district levels and below, a large number of governmental on other agencies are involved in rural development. Accordingly, proper and timely coordination of activities by all of them is essential. Yet a considerable segment of official respondents, more than their non-official counterparts have perceived lack of coordination to be problem. This has been so even in west Bengal where the Sabhadhipathi of the Zilla Parishad is treated as the leader of the district and even the District Magistrate has been brought under zilla Parishd by designating him as Executive officer of the Zilla Parishad.

Table 9: Shortage of Funds

S.No.	Response	Bihar		West Bengal	
		Official	Non-Official	Official	Non-Official
1	Yes	24 (80.0)	23(92.0)	15 (60.0)	25 (100.0)
2	No	6 (20.0)	2 (8.0)	10 (40.0)	-
	Total	30 (100.0)	25 (100.0)	25 (100.0)	25 (100.0)

Shortage of funds has been overwhelmingly perceived as contributing factor to the administrative inefficiency, by the non-officials and, to a slightly lesser extent, by the officials. However, the extent of perceived shortage of funds could not be ascertained even during discussion, PR bodies are autonomous and their 'autonomy depends upon the extent of their financial independence. In the interests of autonomy and accountability and promoting responsibility and judiciousness in expenditure, it is desirable that devolution of funds to the PR bodies from higher levels of government is linked and related to the self-efforts of these bodies in raising their own resources from the sources earmarked to them.

Shortage of material leading to work hold-up has been perceived as an important factor contributing to administrative in efficiency by a majority of officials and non-officials in West Bengal and by a majority of officials in Bihar. This factor is also linked, to some extent, to the lack of coordination discussed earlier.

Table 10. Shortage of Material

S.No.	Response	Bihar		West Bengal	
		Official	Non-Official	Official	Non-Official
1	Yes	27 (90.0)	6 (24.0)	14 (56.0)	13 (52.0)
2	No	3 (10.0)	13 (52.0)	11 (44.0)	12 (48.0)

3	NR/DK	6	-	-	-
	Total	30 (100.0)	25 (100.0)	25 (100.0)	25 (100.0)

The explicit objectives of decentralized democratic institutions ca be listed. These include, among other things, a greater administrative efficiency, greater accountability to the people, more realistic planning reflecting local needs and conducive of equitable distribution of benefits of development, better implementation of development projects, a greater participation of the local people in the process of administration and planning and strengthening the power base.

Keeping these basic objectives in view , we sought the opinion of our respondents as to whether these bodies achieved the objectives. The responses are tabulated below.

Table 11: Whether PRIs Have Achieved Their Objectives

S.No.	*Response*	*Bihar*		*West Bengal*	
		Official	*Non-Official*	*Official*	*Non-Official*
1	Fully	3 (10.0)	17 (68.0)	5 (20.0)	19 (76.0)
2	Party	15 (50.0)	4 (16.0)	20 (80.0)	5 (20.0)
3	Not at all	12 (40.0)	-	-	-
	Total	30 (100.0)	25 (100.0)	25 (100.0)	25 (100.0)

Ten percent of the officials from Bihar and 20 percent from West Bengal have felt that the objectives have been fully achieved. Fifty percent of the officials in Bihar and 80 percent in West Bengal considered that the achievement has been only partial. But both in Bihar and West Bengal, a majority of non-officials have considered the objectives to have been fully achieved.

Presumably, this favourable response has been promoted in the non-officials by their overwhelming desire to ensure the perpetuation of their self-governance that gives them a voice and a position in the community. Despite the positive response of both the officials and non-officials there is scope for improvement in the performance of these bodies. The suggestions of the non-official respondents in this regard are set out in the following Table.

Table 12

Suggestions for Improvement (Non-Officials)

S.No.	*Suggestion*	*Bihar*	*West Bengal*
1	Devolution of more powers	-	8 (32.0)
2	Devolution of more funds	-	4 (16.0)
3	Additional Staff	-	2 (16.0)
4	Vesting of legal power	-	7 (28.0)
5	Creation of District Govt.	4(16.0)	4 (16.0)
6	Making the Institutions operational	21(84.0)	-
	Total	25(100.0)	25 (100.0)

In the case of Bihar, where the Zilla Parishads wer not in operation due to certain legal proceedings, the majority of non-officials pleaded for their revival and reactivation. A few of them desired the introduction of a mini secretariat at district level as an essential adjunct to district administration. Similar suggestion for west Bengal, too, was putforth by a few non-officials of that state. The more pervasive suggestions in West Bengal related to devolution of more powers, more funds, additional staff, and vesting of legal power to deal with matters relating to land acquisition, etc.

As of now, the PR has come to stay in West Bengal

and has been progressively providing effective. The shortcomings in administrative efficiency, resource mobilization, etc., are bound to be overcome, before long, with increased experience on the part of both the public and the government. In Bihar, what is required immediately is the reactivation of the PR bodies through appropriate elections and guidance. The people at large have realized the advantages and utilities of the decentralized system of government in the areas of rural development and are eagerly looking forward to its strengthening. What is needed is to exploit this institutional setting to the fullest benefit of the people for whom it is meant. This will lead to reduction in social inequalities by raising the living standards of the rural poor and thereby enabling them to participate more effectively in the decision–making process.

The point we have tried to bring out, however, is that local government can make a contribution to the development process, if properly endowed and allowed to function. It should be the care and concern of the higher levels of Government to make local governments both self-governments and good governments. The potential of PR Institutions as a contributor to the development process in India remains largely unmapped at present.

Nuances of Participation in Panchayat Raj Framework

The term participation, has assumed greater significance in the contemporary discourse on development although there is no clear cut agreement on its exact meaning, or the way in which the process should be fostered. It is generally asserted that the sources of alternative expoused of the term lie in the basic divergence in perception of the process of development. One interpretation of participation regards it as empowering the poorer sections of the society to take independent, collective and voluntary action in order to surmount their poverty and improve their social status. This paper endeavors to examine the nuances of participation in the broad framework of panchayati Raj.

Lexicographical Meaning of Participation

A common element in the dictionary meanings of the term participation is the focus on sharing or taking part. A variety of nuances like involvement, sharing partaking and a role in decision-making constitute variations on the same theme. But to the extent they are evocative they take us closer to the simulative, political/social science definitions.

Relevance of Simulative Definitions

Simulative definitions are richer in content and more effective in meaning. Carole Patman, for example, visualizes the totality of forms of participation as upward exertions of power by themselves and their superiors. an enunciation in one of the publications of the united nations refers to the creation of an opportunity that enables all members of the community to contribute to the development process and to share equitably the fruits of development, amit Bhaduri and Anisur Rehman see in participation a social experience of sharing in relation to definite social and economic relations. A keener attention to nuances would take us to ideological variation in the liberal socialist spectrum. An important spin-off of the studies on participation could be that in giving insighτs into the dynamics of transition from a relatively more inscriptive traditional base to a more liberal political system. Such a participation is thus, bound to have a vital political dimension. However, the present analysis is content with a subdued attention to the political implications of participation vis-à-vis administration or programme implementation. As pointed out by Montgomery and Esman. Exercising influence on administrative behaviour and the outputs of official actions, has a political dimension. As a point of fact if, we take into account the environmental amplitude of 'control', which occupies a key place in administrative process, participation provides quite a meeting ground between politics and administration.

To sum-up, the political definitions subsume the following components:

(a) Upward exertions by lower rungs:

(b) Access to demand making channels of government bodies; and

(c) Involvement, whether direct or indirect.

Aspects of participation via institution building approach touch participation at numerous points. They may be classified as:

(i) Electoral and operational dimensions of PRIs and cooperatives as vehicles of democratic process; and

(ii) Extorting influence by beneficiary/client groups on the direction and execution on rural development programmes with a view to enhancing their well-being.

Evolving an operational definition of participation out of this welter of evocation meanings is by no means easy. The situation is further complicated by the means or outcome question. Development experts in recent times have been asking for participation in development both as a means and as an outcome. In this context, it would be useful to recall the four–fold classification of Cohen and Uphoff, viz, *(i)* in decision making; *(ii)* in implementation; *(iii)* in benefits; and *(iv)* in evaluation.

Ramesh Arora ably captures the inner dynamic or their interface when he says:

> An active participation would not simply ratify but in fact influence the administrative behaviour and the outputs of official action.

Before we arrive at an operational definition of participation, it would be useful to list out the components which span quite a spectrum of nuances.

These include:

(i) Upward exertions of power by lower, rungs regarded as legitimate by themselves and those above:

(ii) Access to demand making channels of government bodies.[7]

(iii) Involvement, whether direct or indirect (but preferably direct) in processes resulting in the determination of social goals;

(iv) Exerting influence on political and administrative behaviour; and

(v) In the context of rural development, a more effective expression for urges to weaken factors contributing to rural backwardness, including urban clout.

These components, so far as they impinges upon political education conscientisation, and empowerment, chart the path of human resource development. In this sense, the cumulative thrust can be regarded as an end in itself. But the instrumental values of participation are by no means inconsiderable. Its economic content can be said to have the following componets:

(i) Resourse transfers, and sharing in the of economic growth,

(ii) Involvement in decision-making with a bearing on allocation of resourses,

(iii) Development of physical infrastructure through which socio- economic benefits are sought to be realized in the sense that infrastructure connotes shared facilities and amenities in the context of a local community. This might appear to be a little far-fatched we may, however remember that sharing constitutes a core meaning of participation, with involvement being an intimately related connotration, so anything enhancing or reinforcing sharing could be considered an asped of participation.

Aspects of institution building (panchayati raj co-operatives etc.) touch participation, at numerous points. They may be categorized as follows.

(i) Electoral and operational dimensions of PRIs and cooperatives, as vehicles of democratic processes:

(ii) Exerting influence on outputs of official action; and

(iii) Exerting influence by beneficiary/client groups on the direction and execution of development programmes/ projects with a view to enhancing their well- being,

If a concise definition were to do justice to the above components, it might look like:

Participation encompasses institutional and psycho–social processes of development oriented to maintaining and sustaining an atmosphere conducive to higher levels of snaring and involvement in socio–political, economic and administrative spheres on the part of citizens, particularly those belonging to lower, or weaker socio-economic strata.

Some Empirical Glimpses

To illustrate points touched upon above, we are presenting below glimpses from an empirical study conducted a few years ago. Only some broader aspects have been selected for discussion.

There appears to be general agreement that PR has been attending to several different kinds of problems faced by the rural people. Being closer to the grassroots, the PRIs are in a better position to appreciate the problems connected with the local design of life. To a query: how dot he PRIs attend to rural development? The following picture has emerged.

As can gleaned from the above the respondents exhibited a clear understanding of the situation. Further, as one can discern there is no clear concentration on any one of the items listed, which means that there are several aspects that need attention simultaneously.

Communicating development change has become one of the greatest challenges of our times. It does not however mean that change has not taken place, but it has been a slow and agonizing process. It follows that spread of development information has become one of the formidable tasks due to the predominance of traditional attitudes in the society. An important task is to find how responsible are the PRIs in spreading development. Information.

Table 13: Perception of PR Involvement in Rural Development

Construction and Repairs or roads	15 (18.8)	14 (17.5)	18 (22.5)
Construction of Latrines and schools	14 (17.5)	8 (10.0)	10 (12.5)
Spreading messages About RD schemes and participation in them	22 (27.5)	18 (22.5)	20 (25.0)
Supervision of schemes Grounded by DRDA	14 (17.5)	30 (37.5)	20 (25.0)
As elected bodies. PRIs Are useful in resolution of conflicts in the execution of development schemes	15 (18.8)	10 (12.5)	12 (15.0)
Total	80 (100.0)	80 (100.0)	80 (100.0)

Table 14: Role of PRIs in Spreading Development Information

Perceived Role	*IRDP Beneficiaries*	*NREP Beneficiaries*	*Non Beneficiaries*
Effective	63 (73.8)	58(72.5)	66(82.5)
Some what effective	17(21.2)	22(27.5)	14(17.5)
Total	80(100.0)	80(100.0)	80(100.0)

The figures in the table indicate that only a few people among the respondents felt, dissatisfied with the role of PRIs vis-a vis the spread of development communication in the countryside. If late there has been a wide publicity for the programmes meant for the weaker sections. The PR election held in 1987 and 1988 in Andhra pradesh generated great enthusiasm among the rural people. Various political virtually combed the countryside with their manifestoes where they spelt out in detail the lofty programmes they wanted to implement in the event of winning power. Such promises on the poll eve facilitated effective spread of development messages and information in the rural areas.

The bulk of our respondents stated that PRIs were primary established to provide the political expression of the village needs. The basic need of our times is modernization; which can only be realized by the part of state and national leadership. As the lowest rung of Indian polity, panchayati raj is relatively better placed than any other agency, to kindle interest among the rural poor to bring, about, albeit slowly the much needed change, so that the projected transformation can be brought about. A politically articulated rural poor would be self-dependent and can force the leadership to become more responsive as well as responsible. Otherwise, the urban biased ruling elite not bestow attention that deserves on the rural poor, especially their needs, aspirations and problems.

PRIs and Programme Implementation

For IRDP, distribution of loan amount to the beneficiaries heralds the grounding of the scheme. So is the case with NREP when distribution of wages and food grains takes place. A number of evaluation studies on IRDP and NREP have suggested that the PRIs in some states have endeavored to play a more positive role in the execution of these programmes, table 15 presents the position concerning the involvement of PRIs in programmed execution.

Table 15: Positive Role of PRIs in IRDP Loan Disbursement and Distribution of NREP Wages/ Food Grains and Avoiding Delays

Response Pattern	*IRDP Beneficiaries*	*NREP Beneficiaries*
Largely agree	54(67.5)	52(65.0)
Agree	20(25.0)	27(33.8)
Disagree	6(7.5)	1(1.3)
Total	80(100.0)	80(100.0)

A majority of the respondents were convinced that the involvement of PRIs a would help play a positive role in the implementation of development programmes. In the execution of IRDP greater involvement would be pertinent in the market operations such as asset acquisition and sale of the produce of IRDP schemes. Similarly as regards NREP, greater involvement of PRIs would not only lead to the creation of community assets but their proper maintenance too. tn sum, most of the respondents appear to have favored PRIs to perform the role of a watchdog, vis-a-vis execution of development schemes.

To a question who the actual beneficiaries of PRIs are? The following has emerged (table 16)

Table 16: Respondents Perception Regarding the Actual Beneficiaries of Panchayati Raj

Category	*IRDP Beneficiaries*	*NREP Beneficiaries*	*Non Beneficiaries*
Individuals	4 (5.0)	1 (1.3)	11 (13.8)
Specific groups	6 (7.5)	6 (7.5)	6 (7.5)

People in village as a whole	70 (87.5)	73 (91.2)	63 (78.7)
Total	80 (100.0)	80 (100.0)	80 (100.0)

The respondents exhibited greater perpicatity than can be expected of them when a majority reported that the actual beneficiaries of PR are none other the people in the village as a whole. Even though IRDP is based on individualized participation and NREP on community participation, the effect of these programmes on the village community has to be viewed in a holistic context since the sum total of individuals and their well being constitutes the sum mum bonus of village development.

Other Factors Affecting Participation in the Development Process

Various socio-culture factors appear to hinder the participation of rural poor in the development processes. A case in point, as mentioned by the respondents, is the lack or absence of confidence among the poorer sections, in facing the adversaries with equanimity. This can be overcome if the target become economically better off. This may be realized to some extent by actively participating in various development schemes. Hopefully such an experience gives them greater scope to develop self- esteem, which in turn, may give them the requisite confidence to face the societal challenges. It provides the rural poor an opportunity to develop contacts both with the official and non-official functionaries who matter most in the execution of various development programmers.

For any project to fructify, post grounding operations are as important as the pre-grounding exercises. An overwhelming majority of respondents opined that lack of follow-up action was mainly responsible for the tardy implementation of development schemes. One important remedy suggested by few respondents is the organization of rural poor into functional groups so as to enable them to draw the attention of implementing officials as and when required. As one can glean, there have been attempts by the government to implement programmes for groups of beneficiaries. This implementation of a programme titled development of women and children in rural areas (DWCRA) is a case in point.

Currently, popular participation is regarded as one of the ways for empowering the target groups. Various governmental interpenetration are expected to help promote the process of empowering the rural poor, and this might result in transforming the social, economic and political spheres of the society. That apart, active participation enable the participations to wring some barging power with regard to genuine claims vis-a vis the process of development.

Some or all the factors listed above have figured in other empirical studies. One advantage of this Investigation is that the focus on participation with its attendant accent on the political component of development can throw fresh insights and a new perpective, demonstrably useful in appreciating the limitations of the conventional wisdom of administrative functionaries.

Implementation of Rural Development Schemes: A Political Process

In the light of recent socio- political developments, a renewed emphasis on both decentralized planning and revival of PRIs can be considered signboards of an emerging political scenario. Moreover, the planning and implementation of schemes like IRDP and NREP (now JRY)is being in- creasingly perceived as aids to deriving political dividends besides helping fulfil the establishment of a welfare state. The bulk of our respondents too shared this viewpoint. In order to enhance their sway over the weaker sections, the elite groups tend to evince keen interest in the execution of rural development programmes. In such a context, wider participation of the target groups would be a corrective.

Participation

Interface Between Conceptual and Empirical Aspects

Implementation of development programmes like IRDP and NREP is a complex proposition. A narrow administrative perspective will not do justice to a spectrum of psycho–social dimensions. One advantage of examining participation in a participatory perspective is that it invites about either the variables involved or the conclusions arrived at much depends upon how one looks at participation. If one is ideologically pre-disposed to a strong sense of commitment to participation, he would be less attentive to instrumental values. The difficulty would be greater if one is not sufficiently careful about the nuances spanning lexicographical and simulative meanings. Lexicographically, sharing or taking part touches the core of participation. Whereas in the latter sense, propositions subsuming the following classification from the very basis of participation:

(i) Upwards exertion of power by lower rungs:

(ii) Access to demand making channels of government bodies:

(iii) Exerting influence on political and administrative behaviour:

(iv) Involvement in processes resulting in the determination of societal goals:

(v) In rural development context, a more effective expression for urges to weaken factors contributing to rural backwardness; and

(vi) Social experience of sharing in relation to definite social and economic relations.

The data presented in the study are too varied and contextually too closely oriented to administrative aspects to permit neat generalization in terms of any or all the dimensions listed above. Even so, there are certain strands which are discernible fairly clearly. Data involving membership of, or association with, political parties have a very, high salience, similarly PRIs and leaders account for a higher proportion of attention or appreciation vis-a via success in implementation. As is discernible, the respondents are not unfair to officials, they get their due. All the same, the overall thrust of data suggests that democratic processes mediated by structures like political parties and PRIs cooperative contribute to raising their level of awareness pressure for mobility: which happens to be the first dimension in the classification referred to above. From this to the sixth dimension in the classification referred to above.

from this to the sixth item, there is a wide area of overlapping meanings, and actual behavioral transitions or programmes. As our data in different items have different empirical orientation, one may have to resist the temptation to bridge the conceptual- cum-empirical gaps with a facile ideological span. However, there is quite a bit of empirical evidence to suggest that access to demand making channels of governmental structures means a higher, there is quite a bit of empirical evidence to suggest that access to demand making channels of governmental structures means a higher sense of participation in decision-making process: whether passive or indirect in the case of spectators or active in the case of those who might be called gladiators. Certain continuities between the elites and the common people can be postured as the sum and substance of democracy.

In societies less ascriptive than the Indian society, and characterized by visible progress in the direction of socio-economic equality, the psycho-social currents and cross currents and cross currents of the type discussed above would not be new. This would not be so in the case of Indian society, if one is attentive to the massive gap between an ascriptive and a participant society. Against this backdrop, even milder versions of participation in lowest caste-cum–class strata acquire pragmatic significance, and the poignancy of a fresh experience. In the informal interactions of the author with a large number of people, several situations were suggestive of the above picture. Such intimations educate us about the contribution of participation to political education, contribution of the ordinary people to influence locative decisions and resource transfers with a visible bearing on the development of infrastructure—psychic, physical and political. Not the least important aspect of this contribution would be bridging communication gaps between non-official leaders, officials and the beneficiaries.

Concluding Remarks

It is attempted blow itemization of some propositions which may be construed as derivative hypotheses for further research on rural development participation.

1. Common people tend to perceive participation both as a means and as an outcome. The inner dynamic of participation reinforces development. More participation could mean better awareness and a progressive expansion in the horizons of involvement leading to a great sense of process.
2. Participatory structures like PRIs can be visualized as capacity en-hankers as well as gap closers. When one thinks of capacities and gaps. One has to identify the strengths and limitations of the official and elective wings as well as those of the common people who should be increasingly regarded as subjects of development.
3. Programme planning and implementation are more complex propositions than generally proposed, but both will gain in effectiveness if keener attention is paid to the nuances of participation and their orgnisational implications. This also includes software aspects like styles of communication. There is also the adage that local problems have local answered. Both in identifying local problems as well as answers. Participation can be prossedinto service in significant ways. All this does add up to saying

that both the development functionaries—officials and elected representatives—will have to shed elitism, and develop greater respect for the needs, feelings perceptions and wisdom of the common people.

Bibliography

India, Planning Commission, Committee on Plan Projects, Report of the Team for the Study of Community Projects and National Extension Service (Chairman, Balwantrai G. Mehta) New Delhi 1957, see Vol. I.

The Central Council of Local Self-Government, Fifth Meeting, Hyderabad, NIRD, 1959.

M. Shiviah, et.al., *Panchayati Raj : A Policy Perspective*, Hyderabad, NIRD, 1986.

M. Shiviah, et.al., *Panchayati Raj : An Analytical Survey Hyderabd*, NIRD, 1976.

Surat Singh, PRIs – Extent of Coverage, *Kurukshetra*, Vol. XXXVII (6), March 1989, p. 21.

Balwantrai Mehta Committee Report, *op. cit.*, Vol. 1, 2.88.

Panchayati Raj at a Glance, 1989, India, Ministry of Agriculture (Department of Rural Development, New Delhi), 1971.

India, Ministry of Community Development and Cooperation, Report of the Committee on Panchayati Raj Elections (chairman, K. Santhanam), New Delhi, 1965.

India, Administrative Reforms Commission, Report of the Study Team on District Administration, New Delhi 1967, Hereafter referred to as HRC Study Team Report.

Rajasthan, Community Development and Panchayats Department, Report of the High Power Committee on Panchayati Raj (Chairman: Girdharilal Vyas), Jaipur, 1973.

ARC Study Team Report.

Narsimham Committee Report.

Maharashtra, Rural Development Department, Report of the Committee on Panchayati Raj (Chairman: LN. Bongirwar), Bombay, 1971.

B. Maheshwari, *Studies in Panchayati Raj*, Delhi, Metropolitan, 1963.

John K. Galbraith, *The Nature of Mass Poverty* (Cambridge Mass : Harvard University Press, 1979), pp. 52, 57 & 58.

Albert Hirschman, "The rise and Decline of Development Economics", *Development: Seeds of Change* (theme : "Limits of Economics), 1986 (3), pp. 8 & 9.

Ronald A. Wykstra, *Introductory Economics* (New York: Harper & Row, 1971), p. 610.

Amartya Sen, Resources, *Values and Development* (Delhi: Oxford University Press 1984), pp. 529, 514, 504 & 517.

Quoted in Norman D. Palmer. "Development : The Need for an Effective dialogue," in S.K. Sharma (ed)., *Dynamics of Development : An International Perspective* (Delhi: Concept Publishing Company. 1977), p. 97.

Ignacy Sachs, *Studies in Political Economy of Development* (Oxford: Pergamon Press, 1980), p. xi.

Vide Paras 5,6 & 7 of the Resolution., M.Venkatarangaiya and M. Pattabhiram (ed)., *Local Government in India –Select Readings* (Bombay : Allied, 1969), pp. 108-110.

Young India, 29.01.1925.

Harijan, 01.07.1947

Jawaharlal Nehru's Speeches, Vol. IV (New Delhi : Publications Division), pp. 92-94. From Speech at Nagaur, Rajasthan, on the occasion of the inauguration of Panchayati Raj. October 2, 1959.

Quoted in S. Gopal, Jawaharlal Nehru : A Biography, Vol. III. Message on the first anniversary of the inauguration of Panchayati Raj in Andhra Pradesh.

B.C.Smith, *Decentralisation : The Territorial Dimension of the State* (London: George Allan & Unwin, 1985).

C.B. Doob, *Sociology : An Introduction* (second edition, Holt Rinehart and Winston, Inc. New York (1988).

B. Sarveshwara Rao and K.V. Ramana, 'Panchayat Samitis: A Case Study in Andhra pradesh," G. Jacob (ed) *Readings on Panchayati Raj* (National Institute of Community Development, Hyderabad, 1967).

B. Maheshwari, *Studies in Panchayati Raj* (Metropolitan, Delhi, 1963).

Roy, Bhakta Pada Sinha, *Panchayati Raj and Rural Development*, (Abhijeet, Delhi, 2008).

Roy, Dipen, *Finances and Accounting of Panchayati Raj Institutions in West Bengal*, (Abhijeet: Delhi, 2005).

M.V. Mathur, Iqbal Narain, V.M. Sinha and Associates, *Panchayati Raj in Rajasthan: A Case Study in Jaipur District*, (Implex India: New Delhi 1966)

P.N. Sheth, "Panchayats, Politics and Social Change," *Vidya* XI-1 (Jan.1968)

V.M. Sirsikar, *The Rural Elite in a Developing Society* (Orient Longmans, New Delhi, 1970)

V.G. Nandenkar, *Local Government: Its Role in Development Administration* (Concept Delhi 1979).

N.R. Inamdar, *Functioning of Village Panchayats* (Popular, Bombay 1970) pp 45-66 177-191.

H.J.Pandya, Leadership in Panchayati Raj- its Composition and changing pattern (Mimeographed) (Department of Public Administration, South Gujarat University Surat 1974)

Maharashtra Rajya Zilla Parishad va Panchayati Rajya Parisamvada (in Marathi) (Gokhale Institute of Economics, Pune 1963).

Index

A.D. Gorwala Report 108
Administrative Reforms Commission 10
All India Educational Survey 98
Amit Bhaduri and Anisur Rehman 150
Antyodaya 114
ARC Study Team on District Administration 9-11, 108
Arora, Ramesh 152
Ashok Mitra Committee 108
Asoka Mehta Committee report 85, 113-14, 120, 132
Balwantrai Mehta Committee 6, 8, 112, 132, 134
Balwantrai Mehta Report 1, 85
Bombay Village Panchayat Act 128
Bongirwan Committee 12
Central Council of Local Self Government 2
Chandrakar Committee 108
Cohen and Uphoff 152
Cole. G.D.H. 58
Command Area Development Programme (CADP) 114
Committee System 14-16
Congress MPs' Study Team 14
CPI(M) 122
Daly, Janet 73
Desert Development Programme (DDP) 115
Development of Women and Children in Rural Areas (DWCRA) 115, 159
Dimock, Marshal E. 60
DRDA 140
Drought Prone Area Programme (DPAP) 115
Employment Crying for Panchayati Raj 31-42
Food For Work 114
G.V.K. Rao Committee 86

Galbraith 50, 52
Gandhi, Mahatma 25, 27, 29, 56, 62-63, 93-96, 98
Gandhi, Rajiv 71-72, 110, 125
Gandhian approach 93-96
Gandhigram Rural Institute 100
Gant, George F. 60
Glembiewski, Robert T. 60
Goulet, Denis 52
Gupta era 126
H.C. Mathur Committee 108
Hanumanthaiya Commission 108
HCM Rajasthan State Institute of Public Administration 110
High Yielding Varieties Programme (HYVP) 114
Hirschmand, Albert 51
Integrated Rural Development Programme (IRDP) 114, 116, 122, 141, 157-58, 160
Intensive Agricultura District Programme (IADP) 114
Intensive Agriculture Area Programme (IADP) 114
Jawahar Rozgar Yojana (JRY) 115, 122
Kernaghan, Kenneth 71
Kithara, R. 65
Kothari Commission 100
L.M. Singhvi Committee 86
Laski, Harold 59
Levina, Herber M. 59
Local Level Planning in India 85-88
Local Planning for Educational Development 96-100
Luke, David Fashole 72
Maharashtra Act, 1962 11
Marx 79
Mathur, Harimohan 71
Minimum Needs Programme 115
Montgomery and Esman 151
Myrdal, Gunnar 53
Narasimham Committee 11
Narsingh Rao Dixit Commission 108
National Research Data Management System (NRDMS) 39
National Rural Employment Guarantee Programme (NREGP) 115
(The) Nature of Mass Poverty 50
NCERT 98
Nehru 27-28, 56
NREP 119, 142, 156-58, 160
NSS 35
Organization Structure 2-5
Panchayati Raj, Coverage of 5-6
Perception About Panchayati Raj 139-49
Planning Process 88-96
Planning Commission 1
Planning for the Village School 100-04
Porter and Olsen 72
PRIs and Programme Implementation 156-58
PRIs, Composition of 7-12

Rajasthan Panchayat Act, 1953, 8, 15
Ramchandra Reddy Committee 108
Reddy, Rami 14
Review of Rural Development 129-37
Ripon 51, 54
RLEGP 119, 142
Roy, Raja Ram Mohan 54
Ryotwari system 127
S.G. Barve Committee 108
Sachs 52
Santhanam Committee on Panchayati Raj Elections, 1965 9
Sen, Amartya 52
Sharpe, L.J. 76
Staffing Pattern 12-14
Swami Yatishwarananda 48
Swaraj 25
Toffler 74
Training of Rural Youth for Self Employment (TRYSEM) 114
Tribal Area Development Programme (TADP) 114
UN 102
Uniyal, Lalit 61
Vellodi Committee 107
VLW 13
Vyas Committee 9-10
West Bengal Panchayat Act of 1974 4
Wildausky, Aaron 54
World Commission on Environment and Development 74
World War, Second 127

■■■

